FROM PATROL

D0051634

TO PROFILER,

MY STORIES FROM

BEHIND THE

YELLOW TAPE

CRIME SEEN

DO NOT ENTER DO NOT ENTER DO NOT ENTER
DO NOT ENTER DO NOT ENTER DO NOT ENTER DO NOT ENTER

CRIME SEEN

FROM PATROL COP TO PROFILER, MY STORIES FROM BEHIND THE YELLOW TAPE

KATE LINES

VINTAGE CANADA

VINTAGE CANADA EDITION, 2016

Copyright © 2015 Decentia Consulting Inc

Published in Canada by Vintage Canada, a division of Penguin Random House Canada Limited, in 2016. Originally published in hardcover in Canada by Random House Canada, a division of Penguin Random House Canada Limited, in 2015. Distributed in Canada by Penguin Random House Canada Limited, Toronto.

Vintage Canada with colophon is a registered trademark.

www.penguinrandomhouse.ca

Library and Archives Canada Cataloguing in Publication

Lines, Kate, 1956–, author
    Crime seen : from patrol cop to profiler, my stories from behind the yellow tape / Kate Lines.

Includes bibliographical references and index.

ISBN 978-0-307-36314-5
eBook ISBN 978-0-307-36315-2

1. Lines, Kate, 1956–. 2. Criminal profilers—Ontario—Biography.
3. Policewomen—Ontario—Biography. 4. Criminal behavior, Prediction
of—Ontario. 5. Murder—Ontario. 6. Ontario Provincial Police—Biography.
I. Title.

HV7911.L56A3 2016   363.2092   C2014-906389-X

Photo credits: Page 22, courtesy Ken MacPherson; page 94, left, courtesy Crystal Dunahee; page 94, right, courtesy National Center for Missing and Exploited Children; Page 155, courtesy *Orillia Packet and Times;* Page 173, courtesy Sgt Joanne Stoeckl, Rideau Hall © Her Majesty The Queen in Right of Canada represented by the Office of the Secretary to the Governor General (2003).

Book design by Rachel Cooper
Cover images: (front) © Dave Bredeson; (back) © Andy Brown / both Dreamstime.com

Printed and bound in the United States of America

10 9 8 7 6 5 4 3 2 1

Penguin
Random
House

VINTAGE CANADA

CONTENTS

To those who
stood in front of me, beside me and behind me.
I am forever grateful.

INTRODUCTION

A LOT OF WHAT I KNOW about how criminals think and behave I learned underground. During a pivotal and life-changing ten months of my career in the early 90s, my daily routine was to take leave of daylight, fresh air and windows and descend two storeys to the sub-basement of the FBI Academy in Quantico, Virginia. It was there that an ace team of Behavioral Sciences Unit agents taught criminal personality profiling to police officers from around the world.

Going to work underground conjures up notions of secrets and clandestine operations and, in some ways, that wasn't too far from the truth. I was surprised to learn that not so long before my time there, the workings of the unit were kept under wraps from legendary FBI director J. Edgar Hoover, who regarded the emerging field as highly suspect. It was not until his death, in 1972, that the unit was able to reveal what it was up to.

I didn't share Hoover's disregard for the potential of the soft sciences in helping solve crimes. I had been with the Ontario Provincial Police for thirteen years and already had some pretty varied experiences under my belt. Since working my first sexual assault case I'd known I wanted to focus my career on investigating violent crime. If I could tough it out with the FBI, I would go home with skills and knowledge that were cutting edge, and that would help me make a difference in how we tackled the toughest of crimes. With a payoff like that, I could live without daylight for a while. It was the perfect place for me to be.

Each morning my six classmates and I would gather around the large table in our boardroom office to meet with our instructors. In an era when the pressures of police work were rarely talked about, we were first armed with stress management techniques—such as eating well, getting lots of rest, staying fit, keeping in touch with family and friends, and pursuing activities away from the academy—to help ensure our bodies and minds were healthy and ready for what we would be taught. What followed was a crash course in all manner of violent crimes, working on cases that involved bizarre and gruesome behaviours beyond what I could ever have imagined. Some days were like having a front-row seat to the gamut of human misery.

And what we covered wasn't based on dated textbook theory—part of our day-to-day was working on real-time cases that needed every bit of ingenuity and experience we could muster. Our boardroom was often taken over by BSU agents meeting with detectives to discuss their unsolved cases. There were never any easy ones. They wouldn't have come knocking on the FBI's door if they were.

The first few hours of the meetings were usually spent getting all of the details of the case—listening to the officers tell the story of the crime; what evidence had been collected; the results of forensic tests; what witnesses saw or heard; and, of course, what the victim had to say. In most cases though, the victim wasn't alive to tell their side of the story. This is when crime-scene reconstruction kicked in and our search for behavioural clues started. What could the scene tell us about what went on between the victim and their killer? Why this victim? What was the motive?

Sometimes guests were invited to sit in on these consultations, experts such as forensic psychiatrists, coroners, pathologists and even an entomologist who was also an FBI agent. Everyone around the table had different backgrounds that contributed to the discussion, while the BSU agents had the benefit of their research on all types of violent crimes and had interviewed rapists, killers and other violent offenders. Adding that to the foundation of all of the investigative information and personal experiences shared, a profile of the likely characteristics of the unknown offender would emerge along with suggested strategies to move their investigation forward.

I was still getting my footing in the program when a Canadian case came in: a four-year-old little boy named Michael Dunahee, who had been missing for three weeks. The crucial first forty-eight hours had come and gone in this case and my Canadian brothers, experienced as they were, had become tired, frustrated and were desperate for help. They wanted to know what type of person would take a child like this and if there was something more they could possibly do to bring the little boy home. We may have been deep underground, but where we were was definitely the real world, where trying to understand the criminal mind could be a matter of life or death.

A KID FROM ENNISMORE

"You can be anything you want to be. Don't let anybody tell you any different. Now go and clean up your room."

—Jean Cavanagh, my mom

I ALWAYS LOOKED FORWARD TO SUNDAY mornings when Dad and Mom loaded the three of us kids into Dad's '57 Pontiac. It was peacock blue, just like my favourite colour in the twelve-pack of Laurentien pencil crayons. Dad drove us five kilometres to attend eight o'clock mass at St. Martin of Tours Roman Catholic Church. The church was near the top of the hill in the hamlet of Ennismore, Ontario. We sat in the same wooden church pew every week, ten rows up on the left, and right across from the stained glass window of St. Peter. My older sister, Barb, and I were never allowed to sit beside one another. We got into less trouble that way. My brother, Gerry, was an altar boy, so got to do all the fun stuff: carrying candles, fetching water and wine, holding towels, ringing bells and burning incense.

Each Sunday my parents prayed for the sick or the dead or rain for their crops or whatever the need was at the time. I don't remember what I prayed for, except most likely for mass to hurry up and end while I stood, kneeled and sat as required. The best part of the service was the basket collection of the offertory envelopes, because that signalled Barb and I would soon be running down the hill to the four corners of Ennismore to spend our twenty-five-cent allowances. My sister and I were never given our big payout until mass was over so we wouldn't lose it down the heating grate near our pew. Gerry got his money before church because he had pockets in his pants. He'd be down the hill shortly after us. Dad and Mom would talk with other parishioners out front after church and then drive down to pick us up.

There were two small stores to shop in at "the Cross," as they called the four corners. Crough's included the township post office and the older folk usually went there. We younger ones went to Sullivan's as they had a better selection of candy and other treats. Both sold pretty much anything that adults could possibly want. Farmers could buy their overalls and the big blue salt blocks for their cattle; fishermen their fresh minnows and worms; and cottagers and campers all the things they forgot back home. Joe Sullivan ran his store with his wife, Marcella, and often with the extra help of one of the oldest of their fifteen children. That family alone constituted a significant portion of the hamlet's population.

The only items I was ever interested in buying were pop, ice cream and candy. I'd start with a glass bottle of Coke or Orange

Crush, drink it all down in a few gulps and be ready with a loud belch to greet any of the church ladies just arriving through the door. Ten cents down, fifteen to go.

Next I went to the back of the store to the ice cream freezer to select my flavour of Mello-Roll ice cream cone: vanilla, chocolate or strawberry. While eating my cone I would peruse what was always the last and most time-consuming stop, the candy shelves, where I usually opted to spend my last nickel on Dubble Bubble gum. Once when I was probably about four years old I had come to Sullivan's one afternoon with my dad. He and Joe Sullivan were catching up on the township gossip up front by the cash register. I was back a few rows of shelving out of their sight and stuffing my mouth with as many Dubble Bubble as I could get into it, all the while shoving the empty paper wrappers out of sight. Then Dad called for me to come back up to the front because he was ready to go home. I didn't want to get caught with the stolen gum so swallowed pieces of it all the way home. I don't know how I didn't choke to death. When I was old enough to go to confession for the first time, I told Father O'Donoghue about my early childhood crime spree. I got off lightly: one Our Father and one Hail Mary.

The Cavanaghs and Twomeys owned neighbouring farms in the north end of the township. Joe Cavanagh, my dad, was the youngest of five kids and my mom, Jean Twomey, was the oldest of six. Dad brought Mom to live on his three-hundred-acre farm right after they were married in 1949. He was fifteen years her senior. Mom once told me that he seemed like a good man and hard-working and therefore she married him when he asked her.

She said she fell in love with him in the years that followed. Dad worked the farm every day from dawn until dusk, rarely taking a day off. Mom was a part-time schoolteacher, staying home when we kids came along. Gerry arrived in 1950, Barb followed in 1952 and then me in 1956.

I don't have any recollection of playing indoors as a kid. Along with our cousin Carolyn, who lived at the farm next door, we rode horses and even calves and pigs occasionally. We swam in Pigeon Lake in the summer and skated on it in the winter. We'd slide down a large snow-covered hill in one of our farm fields on old waxy cardboard vegetable boxes. One of my favourite activities was walking and rolling across the backyard for hours on top of one of Dad's empty forty-five-gallon oil drums. Trees, haystacks, snow, ice and discarded farm supplies were our playground equipment. We were expected to be at

Gerry, Barb, me, 1957

home for dinner at noon and supper at six o'clock. No exceptions. Parental interaction was required only to tend to injuries or to intercede in skirmishes. (My sister and I never fought with just words. My worst injury was a broken finger whereas my sister had several trips to the doctor for stitches.)

One of the few activities we did with Dad was making maple syrup in our sugar bush each spring. Each day Dad hitched up a team of horses and we would go into the woods to collect the sap. All of it would be boiled down in large iron pots over a wood fire to create the syrup. We kids were given the responsibility of gathering sticks and wood to keep the fire going. It was a long process, but the end result was worth it.

The cattle, pigs and chickens on our farm were slaughtered for meat. We grew our own fruits and vegetables. Occasionally Dad would take a trip into Peterborough to sell some of our produce, eggs or maple syrup. I loved going to town with him in his old '50 navy blue International pickup. It always made me feel special to have his full attention.

Mom was the disciplinarian in the family. Being a teacher, she had a school strap for any behaviour infractions she deemed worthy of corporal punishment, which thankfully I didn't require too often. My father only struck me once. I had been playing in the loft of the barn where bins of grain treated with insect repellant were stored. One day Dad caught me sitting in the grain bin eating handfuls of wheat. I had been told by him many times not to eat the grain. When I saw him I jumped out of the bin and started to run but Dad took a kick at me and caught me in the bum. It didn't hurt a bit but I cried for hours.

When Dad came in from the barn that night, I sat on his knee until it was time to go to bed.

The youngest in the family usually gets fingered as the spoiled one and I have to admit I lived up to the stereotype. When I wanted something my father was a reliable path of least resistance and I can't recall a time I didn't get from him what I asked for. My mother's denial of something I wanted was unequivocal, but only in round one. If I kept nagging and begging she would usually concede. It played in Gerry and Barb's favour to have me as the frontman for any requests on behalf of the three of us. They knew I offered the best chance for success.

I started to go to public school in 1961 when I was five years old going to a one-room schoolhouse about two miles from our farm. Late that fall the school inspector paid a visit and decreed that since I would not turn six years old until January of the following year I was not allowed to continue. Mom home-schooled me during that winter and I likely learned more from her than I would have at school anyway. In my mind she was without a doubt the smartest person in the entire world and knew the answer to every one of my questions.

When I went back to school the following year, they put me into Grade 2 right away. I moved to the new larger St. Martin Catholic Elementary School in the village of Ennismore the following year. I was a good student and the only times I got into trouble were for talking in class or walking down to Sullivan's store at lunch hour without permission. My punishment was always standing in the hall while class was on. I'd say the rosary until I was let back in. I'd got the hang of proper praying by this time and it was a good way for a Catholic kid to put in the time.

My mother was the one who taught me to read and to love books. My earliest recollection of books is the Nancy Drew and Hardy Boys series, read late at night under the bedcovers with a flashlight. Girl detective Nancy did as good a job as the boys to solve these detective mysteries with good always triumphing over evil, but handsome, blond-haired Joe Hardy was my favourite.

I had to be bused into the city of Peterborough to attend Crestwood Secondary School. Since the bus ride was two hours each way, when I turned sixteen my parents usually gave me their car to drive. I was one of the few students who had a car and on more than one occasion my morning route was diverted to pick up friends and head for a day of sunbathing along the Otonabee River or shopping in Toronto. I became quite proficient at signing my mother's absence notes to get me back into class the next day.

Like many of my schoolmates I experimented with the relatively new phenomenon of soft drugs, like marijuana and hashish, available for purchase in the schoolyard. In Grade 11, a local police officer came to my law class to give a presentation on the dangers of drug use. He cautioned us that there were particular drugs on the streets at that time that were making kids really sick. He wasn't judgmental and didn't lecture us on what we could or couldn't do. The officer just wanted us to be safe and he left a positive impression on me.

During the summers when I wasn't going to high school or later attending university, I did some waitressing and for several summers worked at a camp ground and trailer park on Buckhorn Lake, not far from our family farm. I looked after the small convenience store that was always stocked with lots of penny candy, chocolate bars, gum and soft drinks. I ensured that it was all kept in the shelves right in front by the cash register so that it was always in my sight. As a rehabilitated criminal, I knew what my high-risk items were.

When I finished high school I thought I wanted to be a lawyer. My grades clearly showed I was not a cerebral type but I did make the minimum entrance mark to attend the University of Toronto at the Erindale College campus in Mississauga. My parents were rich with love and support but there wasn't a lot of extra money for school tuition or living expenses for the campus townhouse I shared with five other girls. Student loans, grants and working as a surveyor's assistant at nearby construction sites got me through.

As I approached the third year of my General Arts program I realized that my interest in playing a variety of university team sports, as well as being a little overactive in the extracurricular activities of college life, didn't leave me with the greatest academic standing to apply for law school as I'd hoped. My college roommate had a cousin who was a police officer and I talked with him a few times about his work. It sounded interesting. I'd taken a number of psychology and sociology courses and particularly enjoyed the study of human behaviour. In early December of my graduating year I applied to one of the local police departments and attended their headquarters to take

University of Toronto graduation, 1977

some tests. Before I left I was told I had performed well on all, but a psychological test that apparently assessed behaviour and personality traits had not yet been marked. On Christmas Eve that year I got a letter in the mail to say I hadn't passed the psychological test.

My mother encouraged me to not give up and suggested that I talk to a friend of hers whose deceased father had been a member of the OPP. Her friend offered to set up a meeting in Toronto so that I could meet a friend of her father's who was still an officer. I took her up on the suggestion and met him at OPP headquarters in Toronto for about an hour, and at the end he too encouraged me to give them a try. (It was some time before I realized that my mom's friend's dad was former OPP commissioner Edwin McNeill and the man she sent me to see was Assistant Commissioner Clive Naismith, in charge of Staff Development Division, which included recruitment.) I was twenty-one when I, along with 2,400 others that year, put in my application to the OPP. I completed the same psychological test I had taken before and this time passed it, along with all the other tests.

One of the last phases of the OPP's selection process was a character investigation, which included a home visit to interview my parents. I happened to be at home when the uniformed officer stopped in unexpectedly. I eavesdropped on what my parents had to say, which was very supportive. Before the officer left I asked to speak to him privately in the kitchen. I remember he was leaning against the refrigerator and I was leaning against the stove across from him. I asked him a couple of general questions about the OPP and then I got up the courage to ask him what he thought of women being police officers.

"Honestly?"

"Honestly."

"I don't think you have any place being an officer in the OPP. I don't think any women do."

"Really?"

"Really. But it is just my opinion."

"I hope, if given a chance, I can prove you wrong."

My heart sank. And then he left. To be fair, I *had* asked him to be honest.

A couple of weeks later I got another letter in the mail. I thought I knew what it was going to say. Thankfully I was wrong. I had been successful in my application and was to report for duty at the OPP training academy in Toronto on Monday, July 18, 1977.

HIGHWAYS, TRAGEDIES
AND MIRACLES

*"Choose a job you love, and you will never have to
work a day in your life."*
—Confucius

I HAD THREE WEEKS OF ORIENTATION training at the OPP
Academy on Sherbourne Street in downtown Toronto. Although
about fifty women had already been hired by the OPP since
1974, there was no uniform available in my size. Until one could
be made, I wore men's extra-small blue shirts and pants that I
had to cinch up so much at the waist that the red stripe down
the sides spiralled around my legs. My days were filled with
learning provincial and federal laws, self-defence, firearms and
marching. It all came fairly easy to me except the last as I was
prone to lapsing into a ridiculous-looking "bear walk" (swinging
the same arm and leg at the same time). Thankfully I mastered
it by the time I graduated and even made it on to the class drill

team. There were two other women in my class of forty, although one resigned soon after our initial training. The remaining woman, Sue Lloyd, the daughter of a police officer, was someone I clicked with right away. Sue had been a civilian office assistant with the OPP for several years before joining the uniform ranks so was able to fill me in on what she knew might be in store for us.

My new recruit posting was Port Credit detachment just west of Toronto. It was a "traffic detachment," meaning that my duties would consist primarily of patrolling two of the busiest highway corridors in North America, the Queen Elizabeth Way (QEW) and Highway 401. Both of these highways were policed entirely by the OPP, with Port Credit detachment responsible

My first day in uniform with my niece, Tracy, 1977

for the portion that passed through the city of Mississauga and the west end of Toronto.

I arrived for duty at the detachment on August 9, 1977. My coach officer was Rick Walsh, a last-minute replacement as the previously assigned officer claimed that coaching a female rookie would create too many problems at home with his wife. Rick was thirty-two years old and in great physical condition. He'd been married for eight years and I was thankful to hear that his wife had no issue with him coaching me. For the next several months Rick instructed me on the practical aspects of policing as we patrolled the highways each day.

Rick clearly loved his job and I soon fell in love with it too. I found that our black and white car was a welcome sight to those involved in collisions or breakdowns. It was, of course, a different reaction when we pulled over drivers who'd been speeding or driving under the influence.

Rick instilled in me the importance of being a professional just as much off duty as on duty. He insisted that I attend the monthly off-duty shift parties ("choir practices") that began at eleven o'clock after we finished our last afternoon shift. He told me it was important for a new rookie, especially one of the few women on the job, to attend work functions, have a drink with the boys and be a part of the team. Of course he was right and I became part of a shift that spent much of our off-duty time together. That shift became like family to me. One shiftmate, J.D. Cromie, actually did become a member of my family. He was a Breathalyzer operator, had the easygoing personality required for that job, and after being friends for a few years I decided to introduce him to my sister. Not only did they get married, they stayed married—a significant achievement in my profession.

Shift work wasn't an easy adjustment for me. I'd eaten my fair share of donuts, but I'd never developed a taste for coffee that the other guys drank so much of, particularly on night shift to help keep them awake. When the highways were quiet in the early-morning hours, Rick and I often sat at the side of the road in our cruiser and reviewed various criminal and provincial statutes that I needed to know. If he was driving and I happened to fall asleep in the passenger seat, he would sometimes drive off the highway and deep into a residential area. He then would wake me and tell me that if I was going to fall asleep, I had to take over driving and find my own way back to the highway.

My boss, Corporal Ted Stanford, was fifty years old with a head of thick white hair and salt-and-pepper moustache. Ted had three daughters and seemed to take me under his wing as his fourth. He had worked almost his entire career at Port Credit detachment. He was a kind-hearted, gentle man who took pride in having a shift of young, keen officers who needed no prodding to get out on the road and get the job done.

Ted even had some sympathy for the new rookie who had trouble staying awake on midnight shifts. I never had much of an appetite for eating lunch at three or four in the morning like the others on my shift, so I'd usually have a nap on the sofa in the women's washroom. Ted's office was directly across the hall from it. He would take note of when I went down and, forty-five minutes later, he'd softly tap on the door to get me back out on the road.

One night some of the guys came in off patrol before I arrived for my nightly nap break and set up a mannequin just inside the door of the women's washroom. The arms were straight out from the sides with a bright yellow motorcycle cop's raincoat overtop. The head was covered with a helmet. When I came into the ladies' room, I had to switch on the light that was usually left on—that should have been my first clue. They heard me scream all the way to the other end of the detachment in the radio room where the guys were eating lunch. I could hear them laughing and a few chuckles came from Ted's office as well. There was no nap that night—I couldn't get my heart rate down enough to fall asleep.

I was soon performing my duties on my own. I met some of the nicest people running radar and when stopping cars for traffic violations. It was always a judgement call on what the best method was to deal with poor driving behaviour. A warning often seemed most appropriate. A small few didn't seem to realize that calling me a "pig" or "bitch" was a sure way of earning them a ticket. But more often than not, I handed out tickets with people thanking me and telling me to have a nice day. I treated everyone with respect and almost all returned it back. One memorable exception was an evening when I got sucker-punched while arresting a drunken male pedestrian playing chicken with the traffic on the QEW. My pride was hurt more than anything. Thankfully Rick was with me and along with the help of two motorists we had stopped for driving infractions my roadside wrestling match was brought to a quick end. (All the two drivers received from me that night was my deepest appreciation for their assistance.)

I always wanted to treat people fairly. One early morning I was just about to finish my night shift when a car ran a red light right in front of me. I went after it and, when stopped, asked the driver my usual request for "driver's licence, ownership and insurance, please." As the driver complied, he told me he was dealing with some health issues, the breakup of his marriage, problems at work, and on and on. He even became tearful. I expressed my condolences for the difficult time he was having—but he got a ticket anyway. His sad tale just didn't quite ring true to me.

At a friend's house party in Toronto a few weeks later I joined a small group of people I didn't know. One of the ladies was saying that a guy she worked with always used a "big sob story" when he got caught by the cops for doing something wrong. Apparently he never got charged because the cops always felt sorry for him. But a couple of weeks ago he came in to work outraged that he'd gotten stopped by some bitchy female cop after blowing a red light. For the first time the story didn't work and he got a ticket. I just smiled.

One hot summer afternoon another officer and I were catching up on some paperwork in our air-conditioned detachment office. We were dispatched together to get out on the road right away and observe for a bank robber. A zone alert had been issued giving his and his vehicle's descriptions and that if stopped to treat him as armed and dangerous. As was standard procedure in such calls, we took a shotgun with us and stowed it in the trunk.

We weren't out on the road long when we saw a car that matched the description driving on a four-lane street. We turned on our gumball-red roof light and siren and the driver pulled

Standing: Bruce Pritchard, Ross O'Donnell, Mike Watters, Chris Newton, me, J.D. Cromie, Rick Walsh, Ted Stanford, Roy Wilkinson; Seated: Ken MacPherson

over onto the shoulder of the road with us pulling in behind him. When I got out I grabbed the shotgun out of the trunk. As often happened, rubberneckers slowed down traffic to a crawl. My partner came up to the vehicle on the driver's side and I proceeded on the passenger's side. As we got closer to the car we both realized at about the same time that it didn't exactly match the car description we were given, nor did the driver match the bank robber's description. My partner spoke to the driver through his open window to explain why he was stopped. The passenger-side window was up so I opened the door to add my apologies. As I was opening it the driver yelled, "No!" just as six very expensive-looking Siamese kittens jumped out and scampered past me down into the ditch.

With the shotgun still tucked under my arm, I went after the escapees, calling, "Here kitty, kitty." Unfortunately with the heat all the cars going by had their windows down and could no doubt hear me—I can't imagine what they thought was going on. I was finally able to gather up all of the kittens and return them to their relieved owner. After returning the shotgun to the trunk, I got back into the cruiser and said to my partner, "Don't say a word. Just drive."

Ontario was the first province in Canada to require vehicle occupants to wear lap seat belts. Even though the law had been in force for several years when I became a police officer, there was poor compliance. Many times I gave a warning about a traffic infraction, but rarely passed on the seat belt violations. I had seen first-hand too many serious injuries or deaths resulting from people not wearing their seat belts.

The scene of a traffic accident was the one place that people were usually happy to see me. I responded to one where a young family on a camping vacation was rear-ended by a speeding car. Their eight-year-old son in the back hadn't had his seat belt on. His parents had not moved him since the crash and were frantic when I arrived. I found him crumpled up on the floor of the back seat. His back and legs were badly injured from the impact. The father told me and the ambulance driver, "The sound of your sirens was the sweetest sound I have ever heard." Sadly, from what I saw, I don't think the boy would ever walk again.

When we uniformed police officers had to awaken families in their homes in the middle of the night, we were well aware that our presence would be far from welcome. The OPP delivered news not only of traffic fatalities, but also those relating to homicides, suicides and accidental deaths. When we knocked on the door they immediately knew it wasn't going to be good news.

You could never anticipate what the response to the bad news would be. One thing that was likely was that they would remember every detail of what you said to them for the rest of their lives. You had to be very clear that given what you knew to be true—you were certain that it was their loved one that had died. Some wanted to think it was somehow a mistake but you had to tell them the cause of their loved one's death and the circumstances as best you could. With encouragement, most would contact another family member or friend to come and be with them. We always sat with them until they arrived. It was the worst-possible assignment and you wanted to do your best-possible job.

On one occasion I was the lead investigator in a fatal single-motor vehicle collision. It occurred at about 1:30 a.m. on a fairly quiet stretch of highway. I was on patrol in the area when I got a dispatch call for a 10–45 (fatality). I was there within minutes. Pieces of the car were strewn about on the highway and in the ditches. The largest piece was the rear axle and an attached portion of the trunk. The partially decapitated body of a male driver, of what was once a Chevrolet Camaro, was in the grass median. Witnesses said this car and another one seemed to have been racing down the highway at speeds likely in excess of 160 kilometres per hour. The Camaro driver lost control and hit a series of cement bridge posts, breaking further and further apart with each impact. The other driver never stopped.

Rick and several other officers attended the scene to assist me with interviewing witnesses and taking scene measurements and photographs. I obtained the dead man's identification from his jeans pocket and realized his home address was just a few kilometres away. He was three weeks shy of his twenty-first birthday. The coroner arrived and officially pronounced him dead. A funeral home came to collect the body.

It was then time for the horrible task of visiting the residence listed on the driver's licence. I asked Rick to come with me and we arrived at about 3:00 a.m. We parked in the driveway and went to the side door where a light had been left on, probably for the young man we had just left. I knocked several times and a middle-aged man answered the door. I introduced myself and Rick and requested that we come inside. I asked him if he knew the name of the young man and he said that he was his father. I asked him if he was alone and he said that his wife had just been awakened as well. I asked him to get her as I wanted to talk to them together. The two returned, both still in their pajamas, and I told them the news that their son had been killed in a car accident. They said they had just seen and talked with him a few hours earlier. I told them again that I was sure it was him. The young man's father just stared at me in disbelief. His mother became hysterical and inconsolable. We encouraged the father to call a relative, which he did. Through his tears, he asked a few questions about how the accident occurred and I told him what few details I knew. I dreaded that either of them might ask if they could see their son and his mother eventually did. I was at a loss for what to say, responding only that it was not possible at that time. We waited with them in the living room for the arrival of other family members. It was gut-wrenching. After their relatives arrived Rick and I excused ourselves, letting them know we would return later in the morning.

We attended the hospital morgue to view the body and were then sure that the confirmation of identity that was required would be impossible through any facial recognition. When we returned to check in with the family we found a cousin there who was agreeable to accompany us to the morgue to spare the family the task of identification. On the way to the hospital we explained the circumstances. He advised us that he had spent many summers at a lake swimming with the deceased and knew that he had several birthmarks on one shoulder. At the morgue the body was draped in a sheet. Rick and I stood on each side of him, holding him steady. The sheet was pulled back to show the shoulder area and he was able to identify the birthmarks as those of his cousin. He was very distraught afterwards, but acknowledged he was glad that it was him that came and not the parents. We returned him back to the home. I had been putting off the one last conversation that I had to have before I finished my shift. I spoke with the father privately, hoping that somehow having had a few hours to have the initial shock sink in, he would now be able to cope with the further details of his son's fatal injuries. Or maybe it was just me needing the time to get up the courage to tell a father that he would not be able to see his son's face one last time. Those were the worst few minutes of my life.

And then, after seventeen hours of work, I went home and cried myself to sleep.

In 1979 I was living on the eighth floor of a condominium in Etobicoke, west of Toronto. On November 10 I was home all Saturday evening and turned off my television just before midnight. I didn't want to stay up too late as I was starting day shift the next morning. As I shut my bedroom blinds, I glanced out the window and saw the orange glow of what seemed to be a large fire in the west, about ten kilometres away. I drifted off to sleep thinking my fellow emergency responders in the Mississauga Fire Department likely had a long night ahead battling some type of industrial fire.

I didn't open my blinds before I left for work the next morning but as I drove toward the office I could see smoke still billowing from the area of the fire I'd seen the night before. When I arrived in the parking lot at work it was full of marked police cars from other southern Ontario detachment areas. Getting out of my car I could smell the smoke and a strong chemical odour. Our small detachment office was crammed with officers and we were soon briefed that at 11:53 the night before a train had derailed in an industrial area about five kilometres northwest of the detachment. Part of the derailed load included "dangerous commodities" cars, one being a load of ninety tons of chlorine gas. Forty-five thousand Mississauga residents were already on the move following overnight precautionary evacuation orders. There would be no tickets handed out or arrests made that day, or for the next several days.

During the day stories emerged through the throngs of media flocking to the scene: emergency responders, area residents and curious onlookers had narrowly escaped serious injury from exploding derailed cars leaking flammable liquids and vapours. There were reports that flames from the initial explosions were visible a hundred kilometres away.

Within minutes of the derailment, OPP and other neighbouring police agencies sent officers to respond to the scene. Overnight they assisted Peel Regional Police with the traffic chaos created by evacuated families trying to leave the area, as well as onlookers and media trying to get in. They also helped to cordon off the perimeter of the derailment scene and expanding evacuated areas.

With the confirmation that chlorine gas was now drifting south of the derailment scene, my day shift was dispatched to assist with further evacuations. I was assigned a grid of residences north of the detachment. I had no legal authority to force people to leave their homes but tried my best to persuade them to do the right thing and get their families out of potential danger. (Even today, under the current Emergency Management and Civil Protection Act, there is no authority to force someone to evacuate. The only legal power is under common law and only if there is imminent danger, such as a fire in a residence.)

As I went from door to door, the wind started to pick up and the smoke and chemical smell started to get stronger. I certainly could have used a gas mask but they hadn't been distributed to us. When people answered my knock at their door I'm sure I must have looked like I was crying with my watering, stinging eyes and running nose. Some residents were just getting up and had no idea what had happened. Others were already making plans to leave their homes. I told them what little I knew: that there were dangerous gases on a derailed train and that they needed to leave their homes for their own safety. I had no information as to how long they would be gone. Some needed a little persuasion. Others refused. I asked those that were going to evacuate to leave their front lights on to show they had left.

Evacuation announcements continued in stages throughout the day to mitigate some of the traffic chaos and avoid overwhelming evacuation centres that had been set up. Once my area evacuation job was complete, I was assigned to a roadblock just north of the derailment at the perimeter of the evacuation zone. A crisis can often bring out the best in people and I saw that throughout the rest of the day. Volunteer services, like the Red Cross, St. John Ambulance, Salvation Army and others, were on site quickly. They were able to assist the evacuees to register their whereabouts for inquiring family and friends, as well as provide food, shelter and medical assistance if needed. Stores and restaurants in unaffected areas opened their doors and gave free meals to people in need, as well as to emergency and support personnel. Concession trucks full of food, drinks, candy and even cigarettes stopped at roadblock locations and opened up their doors. Even people in their private vehicles passing by would stop and hand you out something to eat or drink.

Occasionally people would come by looking for their friends or relatives in the evacuated zones and were worried that they may still be inside. It was actually lucky that evacuation efforts took place at night and then over the course of a Sunday. Most parents were in the company of their children and other family members and were evacuated together. If this incident had occurred during a weekday when parents were at work and children were at school or with caregivers, the evacuations would have been much more chaotic.

Such evacuations can run the risk of stay-behind looters. Later in the afternoon I chased down three teenagers in my evacuated zone and escorted them to the perimeter with a "don't come back or else" warning.

At midnight, another OPP officer arrived to relieve me. As I headed south on Highway 10 back to the detachment, it was eerie driving through the deserted main street of what had become a ghost town. After being on my feet for most of the last eighteen hours, I was beat and ready to head to my thankfully non-evacuation-zone home. It had been an exhausting yet exhilarating day on the job playing a very small part in emptying a city of 116 square kilometres.

With just a few hours of sleep, I was back up for Monday's day shift. Recently elected Mississauga mayor Hazel McCallion had officially declared the evacuated areas of her city closed for business until further notice. As I made my way to the office, I was soon part of the traffic chaos created by the QEW closing overnight. Toronto's regional commuter rail transit system in the west end was closed as well. Traffic was gridlock. It would have been much worse if it were not that many commuters were off work for Remembrance Day. That day I was assigned to the north end of our detachment area covering Highway

401, the only other major artery into Toronto that was open to traffic. In the afternoon I was reassigned to another roadblock location. A number of evacuees were making their way back to the cordoned-off areas in which they lived, in the hope that we could assist them in returning to their homes. Most of my day was spent trying to calm down the people who had not yet been given authorization to return to their homes. The only ones who I allowed back in were those that had approval from the emergency operations centre to retrieve necessary medications. Many could not make alternative arrangements because their medical practitioners' offices had also been evacuated.

By Tuesday, chemical experts on site determined that the hole and leak in the chlorine tank was likely caused when it blew open. It seemed the resulting pillar of fire and heat sucked most of the chlorine to such a high altitude that it dispersed over a wide area. Allowed to return home that day were 144,000 evacuees. The rest of the 73,000 evacuees gradually returned home through to Friday as more and more areas were determined to be safe. Thankfully, the QEW was reopened in time for Friday afternoon rush-hour traffic. The city of Mississauga was officially reopened at 7:45 p.m., nearly six days after the derailment occurred. Mayor McCallion said, "If this had happened a half-mile farther down the track—either east or west—we would have seen thousands of people wiped out. It's a miracle it happened here [in an industrial area]."[1]

Many agreed with the mayor that it was a miracle that there was no loss of life and few injuries resulting from an accident of such a large scale. Only one arrest was made during the incident, of a man trying to run a roadblock. At the time, it ended up being the largest peacetime evacuation in North America with over 220,000 people from Mississauga and nearby Oakville leaving their homes. (That record stood until 2005 when close to one million residents evacuated their homes in New Orleans to escape Hurricane Katrina.)

Short-term assignments like assisting with the evacuation provided a welcome break during my four years of doing traffic patrol. I had arrested nearly two hundred impaired drivers and was getting great feedback from my bosses, but the routine was starting to get to me and I had the urge to try something different. Vacant constable positions, usually in small and remote northern Ontario towns, were regularly displayed on the office bulletin board, but I was twenty-five, single and enjoyed the social opportunities I had living in the Toronto area. One day a new position was posted to work in the Toronto office of Special Services Division. They were looking specifically for an unmarried female constable who would have the ability to travel throughout Ontario for two years. I applied and got a job that would never make me feel like I'd had "just another day at the office."

OUT OF THE BLUE

"If you aren't in over your head, how do you know how tall you are?"
—T.S. Eliot

THE NIAGARA FALLS RESTAURANT was a dive just as I expected. When my potential new boss called me on the telephone the day before, he told me he had received my application in the mail. He also said that he could tell by the sound of my voice that I'd likely be good for the job—whereas his voice sounded like he'd just awakened from a three-day whiskey bender. We agreed to meet the next day at two o'clock.

What to wear to a job interview is always a crucial consideration. For this one I went with a low-cut tank top, jean jacket, tight skirt that barely covered my butt, black stockings and black high-heeled boots. I teased my blond hair and piled on the makeup, going heavy on the black eyeliner, red lipstick and nail polish.

I saw a booth in the back of the restaurant and walked past a table with two guys eating lunch. One looked up and smiled as I walked past, but no one else seemed to give me a second look. I sat down facing the wall. Like all cops, I didn't like not being able to see what was going on in a room but today I wanted this guy to come looking for me.

He found me easily enough and looked pretty much as I expected. Short, fat, unkempt. He got down to business right away.

"You Katie?"

"Yep."

"So, why do you want to do this job?"

"I need the money."

"Ninety percent of my customers want to go all the way."

"I got no problem with that."

He asked me if I had a car and told me how he'd assign me my calls, which he said would take me an hour to an hour and a half. It was a cash-only operation, and I'd be busiest between four and eight o'clock. "Weird stuff"—men who were into cross-dressing, for instance—would be twenty-five dollars more. I'd split whatever I made with him. We also covered the price for orgies and how I'd get his money to him. He said if he wasn't at home, to give it to his wife.

The whole conversation lasted ten minutes. He told me he might even have a call for me that night. I slid out of my seat and left, surprised the interview was so short, and relieved there was no request to complete any kind of practical skills exercise as part of his applicant selection process.

I drove for several blocks, making a few turns along the way to ensure the pimp wasn't following me. I turned into the back parking lot of an office complex where I met with my cover team, the two guys who had been in the restaurant. I pulled off my wire from underneath my jean jacket and handed over the evidence they needed. They told me the conversation I'd had sounded good and that I'd gotten them everything they needed. We said goodbye with my promise that I would have my Crown brief statement to them in a few days.

It had been two years since I transferred to the OPP's Toronto Drug Enforcement Section to work as their first female UC (undercover) officer back in 1981. I was sent on courses, conferences and seminars, but it was the guys in the office, who collectively had worked hundreds of UC projects, that taught me how to play the role and how best to protect myself from getting hurt. Part of their practical training was dropping me on a downtown street corner one day and telling me to panhandle to get used to being on the street. I was alone for about three or four hours and collected fifty dollars in small bills and change. I declined one guy's offer to go down a nearby alley with him and get more than pocket change in return. Although they never said so, I had the feeling my big brothers were nearby keeping an eye on me.

It was a world away from the type of work I did in Port Credit where wearing a uniform was usually enough influence to get people to do what you wanted them to do. As a UC, I couldn't carry a police revolver or a billy stick. I had to rely on my personality and all those good persuasion skills I'd learned as a kid to get people to say and do things they would never do if they knew I was a cop. And if problems arose, I'd have to talk my way out of them. I was initially assigned to do a number of "arm piece" roles where I'd accompany a male UC to add to his credibility in an assignment. I would also act as his cover officer, backing him up in case of trouble. Like most UCs in this line of work, I hated doing cover, and loved being the UC.

Most of my assignments required my once-professional image to be downgraded to low class and trashy, with a mouth to match. My beloved designer clothes were pushed to the back of my closet and up front were mostly jeans, T-shirts, tank tops and boots. No brand names or logos allowed. You also needed a good cover story when you were a stranger arriving in a new place. I usually stuck with being an out-of-work waitress or having just been beat up and kicked out by my old man in some other town. I made it a habit of bumming drinks, cigarettes, food and even drugs. If I paid for anything I would always try to negotiate the price down as best I could. Undercover drug purchases were no exception. Since most of my work was in bars, I knew I would be asked in court how much I had been drinking at the time of a UC buy. My drink of choice was Molson Canadian beer in a dark brown bottle. You could nurse it for a long time without people really noticing how much you were drinking.

I was one of the few policewomen in Ontario working undercover at the time. The targets were so gullible that some days it was like taking candy from babies. I never led any of them into thinking that they were going to get something from me other than my cash in return. If they thought any different, too bad for them. One unfortunate cad apparently misunderstood. Months later, when he was being escorted into the courtroom, he told the court officer, "When I gave her the shit, I thought I was going to get screwed. Boy did I get screwed." He gave me a big smile when he saw me in the courtroom gallery and pleaded guilty.

Getting "narc'ed," that is, challenged by someone who thought you might be a cop, was part of the job. I remember a bad guy once telling me that he had never sold drugs to a narc because if you ask them if they're a cop, they have to tell you the truth. I told him I had never heard that before and thanked him for his great advice.

The following was pretty standard for how I dealt with those situations—always with the same opener.

"I heard you got some shit?"

"Yeah. Sure."

"This ain't the same shit that I got off your buddy the other night is it?"

"No it's a lot fuckin' better."

"Yeah that fuckin' shit he sold me was stepped on bad and it's dirty. My friend was up all fuckin' night pukin' after that shit."

"People don't know who you are, eh? So they don't know what to think, eh?"

"I don't really give a fuck what they think."

"I can tell."

"Right on. If those guys don't want to talk to me then fuck 'em."

"It's just that you're a new face. I just thought I'd tell ya so you know what they're thinkin'."

"Well to be honest, I don't give a fuck what they think."

"If you're not all right, don't arrest me."

"Yeah. Right. Like I'm a cop," I laughed. "See ya later."

He was later arrested for selling me speed on several occasions.

I travelled the province working mostly street-level UC projects for other police departments as much as my own. The projects lasted from a few days to a couple of months. I was still single and being away from home for extended periods of time wasn't a problem for me. It could be a lonely existence but I tried to get home as often as I could to be with family and friends for a few days. I had always talked with them about my work when I was in uniform but now I told them nothing about my work as a UC. I don't think they ever would have believed what I was doing . . . or that what I was saying flowed so smoothly out of my mouth.

My workdays were totally unstructured, with little or no supervision. Portraying the illusion of a criminal lifestyle was an important part of integrating into and infiltrating the local drug community. I was vigilant about not getting too attached to any of the people I met. After all, at the end of the project, most would be arrested. I was familiar with some stories of UCs in agencies elsewhere in Canada and the US and even in the OPP who did not adequately protect themselves from "going over the boards" and who got too close to the people they were hanging out with and/or investigating. Their lines between right and wrong got blurred, ranging from inappropriate sexual relations to corruption. The consequences ranged from disciplinary action to criminal charges and dismissal. I wanted no part of that.

One summer I was assigned to work in Wasaga Beach, a resort location on Georgian Bay, with two other UCs, Jay and Cliff. I was really happy to have some company on a UC project for a change. Jay was the first black officer in Drug Enforcement Section, being transferred in at about the same time as I was. Cliff normally worked as a uniform patrol officer at nearby Orillia detachment. He wasn't worried about being recognized while working undercover because most of the population of Wasaga Beach were tourists up from Toronto for summer vacation. We rented a three-bedroom cottage close to the beach. It was a great summer gig for three twenty-something cops.

The guys took turns being the UC lead depending on who made the initial contact with the target. Then the other would act as their cover to ensure the undercover buy went smoothly. My assignment was to be the exhibit officer. The guys would turn their drug buys over to me, I'd bag and tag them, and then take them to the lab for analysis. Given the location, I didn't complain about this back-end assignment. Occasionally I'd step in as a cover officer if one of the guys had a day off or was away at court, so the UC wouldn't be working alone. We spent most of our workdays either in bathing suits or shorts and a T-shirt. Jay looked like a body builder and Cliff was nicknamed "Magnum" in homage to his resemblance to Tom Selleck. The guys weren't hard on the eyes, and most days it seemed I had to run interference to keep the bikini-clad ladies away from them long enough so we could get some work done.

The three of us befriended two local young women who were instrumental in the success of our summer assignment. They had no idea we were cops, just that we were on vacation and wanted to get stoned and have a good time. They were anti-drug and constantly expressed their concern about us being so involved in drugs. However they introduced us to a number of people and we were seen together so much that the drug dealers assumed we had been friends with them for a long time. That facade helped us infiltrate an otherwise tight group of vacationing beach traffickers.

Weekend house parties were common and if we didn't get invited, we'd invite ourselves. One night Cliff brought me along to one in the hope of meeting some new summer residents. We hadn't been there long when a guy walked in and I could tell right away that Cliff was uncomfortable seeing him. Before Cliff had a chance to say anything to me, the guy approached him and asked Cliff where he knew him from. Cliff told him he was positive they'd never met.

When the guy walked away, Cliff grabbed my arm and said, "Let's get outta here." When we were driving back to the cottage, he told me he had arrested the guy a few months earlier after a gas station robbery. Cliff pulled over a car that matched the description that had gone out. He arrested the driver and brought him into the detachment to wait for the other police department to come and pick him up. Instead of putting him in the cells, Cliff stayed with him in an interview room. They chatted for a bit and he eventually confessed to the robbery.

Cliff told me he was amazed the guy hadn't figured out on the spot where he knew him from as they had been in the interview room together for about two hours.

We made more than fifty undercover buys during the two months at the beach including marijuana, hashish, hash oil, LSD, cocaine and speed. At the end of the summer, we held a party at our cottage and invited everyone that we had purchased drugs from. Just about all of them showed up. Over the course of the evening Jay, Cliff and I took turns asking our guests, one at a time, if they wanted to take a walk down to the beach and smoke a joint. Each time just before we got to the beach, a police cruiser would be waiting in the shadows. The officers hopped out, arrested our guests and escorted them to jail. After everyone had left the party, we packed up all of our stuff and moved out of the cottage. We later stopped by the detachment and revealed our true identity to all of our party guests. Almost all pleaded guilty to their charges.

The morning after the project was taken down, I contacted one of the women that we had befriended. She told me she was relieved that we were narcs and not druggies. I was concerned about possible repercussions from some of those arrested, who were friends of theirs. She said not to worry. I kept in touch with both of them for a while to ensure they were okay. No one ever bothered them.

The following summer I was asked to join a Toronto Police Service anti-biker squad investigation into the criminal activities of the Outlaws Motorcycle Club.

Such organizations were extremely difficult to infiltrate but two UCs borrowed from a Toronto drug squad, Bob and Bill, had been undercover for months and were getting deeply involved in the gang. They'd been provided two rebuilt old police Harley-Davidson motorcycles, stripped of all the cop gizmos of course, and looked every bit the part. Given the increasing risk to their safety and to add to their credibility, the guys were looking for two female UCs to partner with them. I wasn't happy doing an "arm piece" role again but I couldn't pass up the opportunity to be a part of infiltrating that sector of organized crime. Beach bars and house parties were a thing of the past. I was now hanging out in sleazy peeler bars and was back into those high-heeled black boots. A black leather jacket was a must wardrobe addition for this job as well.

An officer with Toronto Police, Audrey was selected to join our team as Bill's girlfriend, after the guys found out the club president had a penchant for Asian women. The first morning she came to work I could see Audrey had little experience working undercover. We spent the rest of the day downgrading her wardrobe in Zellers and Kmart stores. I schooled her on her UC role and she was a quick study. Mr. President immediately took a shine to Ling Ling, as we called her, when Bill introduced her for the first time in a Toronto biker bar. Bill also told him he wasn't into sharing. Audrey's and my occasional presence with the guys on the back of their Harleys and hanging out in bars and strip joints seemed to work in increasing their acceptance into the group. Audrey and I eventually branched out on our own, spending time with the bikers' wives, girlfriends and assorted strippers we got to know and we made a few drug buys ourselves.

The four of us shared a crappy basement apartment in the west end of Toronto not far from the Outlaws' clubhouse. We agreed that no one was to be alone in the apartment as the bikers sometimes came by. Our two Harleys were chained to a tree outside at night. I don't imagine the neighbours were too pleased to have us or our occasional unsavoury house guests in their neighbourhood.

One weekend Bob and I travelled in an old pickup truck to spend the weekend with several of the bikers and their wives and kids at a lakeside campground. On that occasion a cover team was sitting out on a boat in the lake some distance away with a set of high-powered binoculars. Bob and I made regular trips to the shoreline so that they could see that we were okay. We were aware by the end of the first day that someone had gone into our tent and pickup truck and searched through our things when we weren't looking. We had been prepared for that possibility and didn't have anything with us that would blow our cover stories.

One night Bob and I were working alone when he got a call to come to one of the strip clubs in the north end of Toronto for an impromptu meeting to buy drugs. We rode up to the club and several bikers met us outside in the parking lot. I started to walk toward the club entrance but one of the bikers told me to stay outside and watch their bikes as they'd had some problems with their bikes getting tampered with in the parking lot lately. I acted annoyed with the request, but what I really didn't like was being a cover officer and letting my partner out of my sight. Bob reiterated for me to wait outside and the look on his face said, "Don't sweat it, I'll be fine." It was a nerve-racking hour while I waited outside, but he finally emerged with a cocaine buy. Sometimes you had to do things that you were uncomfortable with when working as a UC and risk-taking was part of the deal. But I didn't like my job of being a biker broad that night, sitting on a curb for an hour not knowing what was going on with my partner inside. To be honest, I also remember a bout of self-pity wondering why I never got picked for the high-level drug projects where the UCs drove flashy cars, lived in expensive penthouses and hung out in fancy nightclubs.

The guys continued to have success infiltrating the gang and made a significant number of drug purchases. Unfortunately the project came to an abrupt end one night when Bob was recognized at a strip club by someone he had arrested in the past, and he was "narc'ed" in front of some of the bikers. As much as Bob denied he was a cop, he knew the project was over. I wasn't working that night but got a message on my pager to come to our apartment ASAP. Less than two hours later we had police cars standing by outside to make sure no one bothered us as we hastily packed up and moved out. A large bust took place a few weeks later with most of the club chapter members being arrested.

For my final UC assignment, I was working in Kingston keeping company with a police informant. He had made a deal with the local police to get out of some outstanding criminal charges. The police had agreed to look after him if he introduced me around town. I was set up living in yet another dumpy apartment at the edge of town.

The appearance of a long-term friendship between me and the informant assisted my integration into the town's drug scene. I soon became accepted, making friends with the addicts, thieves, hookers, strippers or anyone else who could help me blend in. My daily routine mirrored theirs of walking around town doing nothing or hanging out in bars, playing pool and video games. Like them I was constantly bumming money and drinks, always seeming to be short on cash. To add to my cover story and popularity, I started to sell and give away jewellery I'd claimed was stolen. (A jeweller friend of mine supplied me with the pieces.) It went a long way in my fitting into the city's shoplifting and associated drug culture.

As I became more deeply involved, I was joined by another female UC, Sue, who played the role of my lesbian girlfriend. I was happy to have her company and she also served to put an end to one target I had made several drug purchases from who wanted to take our friendship to the next level.

My last narc challenge happened one night when I had been working in town for a few months. Sue and I were in one of the local bars and she had just left our table to go talk to some people in the billiard room area. I saw a hulking biker type come in the front door and thought he looked familiar. I was immediately nervous because I had just finished working the Outlaws' project in Toronto. I didn't recognize him and he didn't have any colours—no patches on his jacket marking him as a club member. He sat with a couple of guys at a table a few over from me.

I didn't know any of them but I could tell by the way they kept looking over at me that I was being talked about. Suddenly the guy stood up and started walking toward my table. I stood up with beer bottle in hand as he approached. It was the only potential protection I had.

A fellow UC once told me, "If you're ever really nervous, get in real close. Then they can't see your knees shake."

I got in real close and asked him if he was looking for something.

"Nope. Just wonderin' who the fuck you are."

"Why do you care who the fuck I am?"

"People don't know who you are. Maybe you're a narc?"

"Yeah, right, like I'm a narc."

"And if you're a narc, you're dead."

"Well I ain't gonna be dead cause I ain't no fuckin' narc."

Then he just turned around and walked away.

Sue and I had made over fifty undercover purchases of stolen property and drugs and provided intelligence information on other unlawful activities going on in the community. It was decided not long after to take the project down.

I was glad to see the project come to an end. I wasn't enjoying the work as much as I once had and I felt guilty about it. The adrenalin rush of working UC was gone. For the first time in my career I knew I was burned out.

There was also another reason why I felt it was time for a change. In the past I had dated several officers I'd met on the job and was now dating Bob, whom I'd worked with on my previous UC project. It didn't seem to be a problem for him that I was away so much of the time as he was still working long hours as a UC himself. But for the first time in my career I wanted to concentrate on my personal life more than my job.

Once all the arrests were made and my Kingston project was over, Bob and I took a three-week vacation to the United Kingdom to spend some time together. For the most part it was a very relaxing vacation, with one exception. On our last leg of the trip in Northern England, several uniformed local constabulary officers showed up at 6:00 a.m. outside our hotel room door. The officers advised me that I was under investigation for assisting in a prison break the night before. Bob and I gave them permission to search our room and we were escorted to the hotel restaurant downstairs to wait.

An officer eventually came to speak to us. He was full of apologies. It turned out a woman closely matching my description had assisted several prisoners break out of a nearby penitentiary the evening before. Although I knew I had done nothing wrong, it was nonetheless a stressful few hours and certainly eye-opening to experience the other side of the law.

Soon after Bob and I returned home from vacation, I got word that, after several past unsuccessful attempts, I'd finally passed the promotional exam to become a corporal. In 1986 only a few OPP policewomen had been promoted and I took the first position offered to me in Anti-Rackets Branch. Since I'd never really been that good with numbers, it might not have appeared the logical next step in my career, but I was anxious to get my corporal's "stripes." I was assigned to work on cheque and credit card–related frauds, counterfeit currency and later was transferred into the major frauds unit. I struggled with the complex nature of property flips and misappropriations of corporate and government funds, but my co-workers were all supportive. Many took time away from their own cases to help me make sense of hundreds of documents and spreadsheets. Like so many other crime games, these ones were all about manipulating the trust of another. The only difference was that these bad guys wore suits.

I had one break from working these paper-laden numbers cases when I was asked to assist the OPP's Criminal Investigation Branch on a serial sexual assault case. I had never worked on a violent crime case before and jumped at the chance. My job was to re-interview victims in a series of sexual assaults that had occurred in the city of Windsor and other communities in southern Ontario over a period of about five years. The most recent incident had just occurred a few weeks before. The lead investigator wanted me and a woman from the local Rape Crisis Centre to speak with the victims in case anything had been missed earlier. He was also hoping that having two women do the interviews might yield previously undisclosed information.

What made the interviews particularly difficult was the ages of the victims, which ranged from sixty-one to eighty-three. The impact of these types of attacks is severe for any victim, but these older women suffered greatly not only emotionally but also physically. Several were unable to return to their homes after being attacked. One had such an aggressive onset of Alzheimer's disease after she was attacked that she could not be re-interviewed. All of the other women expressed their thanks for us coming to speak with them and said that it had been easier to speak with women, especially about embarrassing sexual details. Visiting them to take their statements was like sitting down with one's own grandmother. Tea or coffee was served, usually along with some cookies. One showed us blankets she was making for her grandchildren to "help her forget." We left several interviews with bags of fresh vegetables from their gardens.

It would not be till 1998, more than seventeen years after the first vicious attack, that a DNA break would finally come in the case, and lead to the arrest of forty-five-year-old Dayle Grayer for four assaults, the last occurring just weeks before he was apprehended. He was later found guilty and declared a dangerous offender, the finding reserved for Canada's most violent criminals and sexual predators, and sentenced to an indeterminate period of incarceration. While justice was done, by that time all but one of the victims had passed away.

In terms of my personal path, that case was a huge turning point—it would inspire me to redirect my career toward working violent crime cases. As horrible as the crimes were, I felt I had helped some of the victims to better cope with what they'd gone through and was also able to collect investigative information that had not previously been known. It was time to go back to perusing the bulletin board for new job postings that could get me into this line of work.

Several months later a new position in the OPP was posted with the successful candidate required to attend a violent crime course hosted by the National Center for the Analysis of Violent

Crime (NCAVC) at the FBI Academy in Quantico, Virginia. The candidate was to have a college degree and superior skills in criminal investigation, verbal and written communications, and had to be willing to attend the course that would entail at least ten months away from home.

Bob was then working full-time for Toronto's anti-biker squad and we'd moved in together. I worried that this time such an extended absence would screw up the first serious relationship I'd ever had. And there was someone else I wanted to keep in my life too. Bob had a teenaged daughter, Cheryl, from his first marriage, and she and I were starting to develop a really great relationship. Although I always thought I'd have kids of my own, my biological clock was winding down and I was running out of time. Cheryl was everything I could have hoped for in a daughter so I was content with the decision that Bob and I wouldn't have any kids together. I worried about leaving the two of them for almost a year but they were both supportive so I submitted my application the next day. I was shortlisted for an interview along with four others. A few days later I got the call and received the news that I was the successful candidate. I was going to be trained to be a criminal personality profiler . . . whatever that was.

EXIT 148

"When you are asked if you can do a job, tell 'em, 'Certainly I can!'
Then get busy and find out how to do it."
—Theodore Roosevelt

ON SATURDAY, SEPTEMBER 29, 1990, I made the ten-hour drive in my unmarked cruiser, south to Quantico. The FBI Academy was about forty miles south of Washington, DC, and inside the one hundred square miles of Marine Corps Base Quantico. It was just about dark when I took Exit 148 off Interstate 95 and drove the last five miles of my journey. The road wound past Marine Corps munitions buildings and long-arm sniper ranges intermittently cut out of dense woods. Several times my headlights lit up the green eyes of wild deer in the ditches, their movements momentarily frozen, as I drove by. I passed a military police cruiser parked on the right side of the road with radar set up and car pulled over. I would come to know they took their base speed limits very seriously.

I wasn't even aware that the FBI had a uniform contingent until I drove up to a checkpoint guardhouse right outside the Academy. A young officer, with "FBI POLICE" on the shoulder of his shirt, stepped out and asked to see some identification and my paperwork inviting me to attend the course. He handed me a parking pass good for a spot in front of my dormitory.

I checked in at the reception desk on the ground floor of Jefferson Dorm. Above the desk was a huge FBI seal hanging on the wall with its motto, "FIDELITY, BRAVERY, INTEGRITY." I received an ID tag giving me access to all the Academy buildings and free dining hall meals. I took the elevator up to the ninth floor and was relieved to find I had a private room and my own bathroom. I took a walk down the hall and found open doors to three rooms occupied by other international police fellows who were taking the same training as me. Two were from Australia state police agencies, Bronwyn Killmier and Claude Minisini, and one from Holland, Carlo Schippers, with the Dutch National Police.

I was impressed and a little intimidated by the amount of violent crime investigation experience my international colleagues had. But what I brought to the table was a different kind of asset: I had wheels. We were about eight miles from the nearest store or restaurant and no one else had a car. It took no persuasion to get them to help me unload my cruiser. They all had arrived by plane with only a couple of suitcases each. I never travel light to go anywhere, except when threatened with an airline fee for extra luggage. My classmates seemed glad about how close my parking spot was to the dorm, since they didn't have very far to lug my suitcases, boxes, hanging bags of clothes, electric cooler, television and bicycle.

The next morning I awoke to the continuous sound of gunfire. Looking out my window, I saw that my room overlooked a multitude of outdoor firing ranges. I later learned that the ranges expended about a million rounds of ammunition a month. There would be no dispute about that number from me.

The four of us international fellows went to breakfast in the cafeteria and then returned to the reception area to meet up with our three American classmates: Paul Gebicke, United States Secret Service; Joe Chisholm, Bureau of Alcohol, Tobacco and Firearms; and Gary Plank, Nebraska State Patrol. Our FBI police

FBI Police Fellowship Graduates, 1991
Front: Claude Minisini, me, Bronwyn Killmier, Joe Chisholm; Back: Paul Gibicke, Gary Plank, Carlo Schippers

fellowship coordinator, Supervisory Special Agent Ed Sulzbach, soon joined us. He was a former New York City schoolteacher who joined the FBI in 1972. Before coming to Quantico, he'd worked extensively in undercover drug investigations and motorcycle gang infiltrations. Ed and I had a lot in common and he assured me that my past undercover work, getting up close to criminal minds, would be helpful to me as a profiler as it had been to him.

The first order of business was for the seven of us to get a tour of the Academy. The original Quantico facility was established in the 1930s and was used just for firearms training. All other FBI training had been conducted in Washington until the Quantico complex of buildings opened on over three hundred acres at the west end of the marine base. The twenty-plus buildings of the Academy were connected by ground-level enclosed glass corridors, a.k.a. "gerbil tubes." A number of times over the next months, I'd be walking in a tube and see a "not so wild" deer grazing just a few feet away and looking in at me. They would not so much as flinch at the constant sound of gunfire all around them.

Ed explained that the students we were passing in the halls included new agents with the FBI and the US Drug Enforcement Administration (DEA). Both groups were at the Academy for several months of basic agent training which included academic instruction in the particular laws they would enforce, techniques of investigation, defensive tactics and firearms training. They both also had rigorous physical fitness programs.

None of them were wearing uniform shirts or stripes down the sides of their pants. Nor did I ever see any of them marching like

I did as a rookie in training. These agents were dressed in uniforms of collared golf shirts, navy blue for FBI and black for DEA, and khakis. Most of them carried briefcases. Some of them even carried laptop computers, which I had never seen before. (I remember saying to Bronwyn that I was confident I could finish my career in policing without ever having to use a computer.) The professionalism required of these new recruits was clearly demonstrated as each time we met one in the hall we were greeted with a nod and "Ma'am" and the men with "Sir." Bronwyn and I joked that it made us feel like a couple of old broads.

In the past the FBI had had a hiring freeze of female agents, thanks to J. Edgar Hoover. Within a few short weeks of his becoming FBI director in 1924, he ordered that the only two women working in the bureau resign. Somehow one female agent slipped through and was hired that same year, but she resigned a few years later. Hoover remained the FBI director until his death in May 1972. Two months later, after forty-four years, women were welcomed into the organization once again.

There were several other groups of students at the Academy at any one time—the largest student body was actually American and foreign police officers participating in a program known as the National Academy. The approximately 250 officers (about 5 percent of them women) were all dressed in red shirts and were there for eleven weeks of academic and physical training.

The National Academy students could take undergraduate and graduate courses in US and international law, forensic science, leadership development, communication, and health and fitness. They were also offered the opportunity to take courses on the application of behavioural science to criminal investigations. I was excited to hear that my group were always invited to sit in on any of the classes. What I ended up learning in those classes would be some of the most valuable training that I'd receive over my entire policing career.

The Academy classrooms were very modern, most in the tiered theatre style. There was also a gymnasium, workout room and indoor pool. The campus started to feel more like a small town when we were shown the library, chapel, bank, post office, dry cleaners and a thousand-seat theatre.

Across the street from the Academy was Hogan's Alley, a mock town built with streets of false-front apartment buildings, stores, a motel, a bank and a real operating deli. Behind the false facades were administrative offices and classrooms. Hogan was the most crime-ridden city in America. Dozens of simulated unlawful activities took place on those streets every day. The FBI and DEA rookies were engaged in practical scenarios to learn investigation procedures and prepare themselves for the real-life world of crime. The "bad guys" were often actors from a local company under contract to the FBI. It was all in a day's work for them to be arrested, searched, interviewed, robbed, assaulted, taken hostage or murdered. Ed warned if something went down while we were walking around on the streets we might be stopped by a rookie and asked to give a witness statement.

The most interesting thing for me in this movie set–like town was the vintage reproduction of the entrance to the Biograph Theater, the famous Chicago landmark. The marquee listed *Manhattan Melodrama*, starring Clark Gable and Myrna Loy. In

1934, FBI agents were directed by Hoover to find John Dillinger, the notorious and vicious criminal who terrorized communities throughout the Midwest of the US in the Depression years. He was wanted on a host of charges including murder, bank robbery and other violent crimes. On the evening of July 24, 1934, FBI agents acted on a tip that their man was at the Biograph watching the famous Clark Gable movie. When he exited the theatre, he realized agents were waiting for him. As he reached for his pistol he was shot dead by the FBI. The event was often described as the beginning of the end of the era for gangsters having a type of hero status in the US.

We went back into the rear of the Academy complex via the gymnasium. Signs nailed to a tree outside the entrance read: AGONY, PAIN, LOVE IT, PRIDE. Ed explained that the messages were in relation to an Academy fitness regimen. A challenging obstacle course undertaken by most National Academy students was a voluntary final test of their fitness before they graduated. The 6.1-mile Yellow Brick Road, built by the Marines, consisted of running, crawling, jumping, scaling and other such maneuvers. Apparently yellow bricks were at one time placed as markers to show the way along the course. Those that successfully completed the course got to proudly display a painted yellow brick as the prize for their achievement. I had no interest in doing the course challenge while I was there because I'd heard there were snakes in the woods and I hate snakes. (That's my story and I'm sticking to it.)

We next stopped by the PX, short form for the military's Post Exchange, which was like a general store with no tax charged.

This Academy PX was full of FBI paraphernalia including grey "FBI Academy" sweatshirts, which were a particularly hot gift item for family and friends back home, especially after being worn by fictional FBI rookie character Clarice Starling in the soon-to-be-released movie *The Silence of the Lambs*. She wore the sweatshirt as she ran through a foggy segment of the Yellow Brick Road in the opening scene of the movie.

Next door was the "The Boardroom," which operated as a coffee shop and fast food restaurant by day and the only on-campus pub by night. Starting that night, I saw that the roughly one hundred Academy students that the room held, mostly men, young to middle-aged, all away from home and ready to let off steam, made for some raucous entertainment by closing time. But it also provided me a great opportunity to socialize with all levels of US federal agencies and cops from around the world. The colourful war stories that were told every night ensured that my learning experience continued long after class hours ended.

From there Ed brought us to where we would study and work for the next ten months. It was located next to our dorm building, but you didn't get to it through a gerbil tube. You went through the Academy's main-level gun vault and firearms cleaning area to get to the elevator. I could smell Hoppe's No. 9 firearms cleaning solvent as we came down the hall.

Even though I cleaned my firearm with that same solvent many times over the years, whenever I got a whiff of Hoppe's No. 9, it always reminded me of walking through the gun-cleaning room that day in Quantico and taking the elevator down to the lowest level in the FBI Academy.

SIXTY FEET BELOW GROUND

"Sometimes the difference between failure and success is a new thought."
—Captain John Cronin, chief of NYPD Bureau of Missing Persons, 1956

A SLOW JERKY ELEVATOR RIDE DOWN two storeys was enough time to hear about how the sub-basement of the Academy was at one time the US government's national emergency relocation centre and, by some accounts, had served as Director Hoover's personal Cold War nuclear bunker. The elevator was so old Hoover must have ridden it himself. (It spooked me that first day, and a few weeks later I got trapped in it for a short time. After that I joined most everyone else and took the stairs.)

The doors opened directly into a reception lobby displaying photographs of the FBI's hierarchy of bosses, as well as five large framed shadow boxes with photographs and police shoulder flashes mounted inside depicting the graduating police fellowship classes that had come before us. Ed explained that in 1984, the year-long program was created to train police officers in crime-scene analysis and criminal profiling. The first year the NCAVC hosted just one police investigator from Baltimore but subsequent years included four to six experienced detectives from across the US. The most recent class included the shoulder flash of the Canadian Mountie Ron MacKay, the first international student who had just graduated a few months before my arrival.

Our shared office was one of about forty rooms in the middle of the underground space. Our work area was a converted conference room with a large table in the middle and desks around the outside. Ed apologized that space was at a premium and that we wouldn't have much privacy but that ended up not being such a bad thing. When agents needed the conference room for a consultation with a visiting police agency, we usually got to stick around. We were allowed to stay and observe the think-tank sessions and eventually even participate. We were often joined in our training and consultation sessions by several other FBI agents undergoing the same training program as we were, adding to the dynamic nature of the atmosphere.

There was a lot of innovative work being done in this subterranean lair. Since the 1960s police officers attending the National Academy had been bringing their unsolved violent crime files to this specialized team of instructors who offered their fresh take on the crimes. The agents, from various academic and investigative backgrounds, worked together to analyze physical aspects of crime scenes in combination with the interactive behaviour between the offenders and their victims. Their brainstorming ultimately resulted in opinions regarding the major personality and behavioural traits of the person likely responsible for the crime. Such predictions commonly included age, sex, race, level of intelligence, criminal history, motive and possible pre- and post-offence behaviours. Initially the agents kept a low profile since Director Hoover seemed to have the same disdain for the use of soft sciences in the FBI as he did for female agents. Their services would not be formally recognized by the FBI until after Hoover's death in 1972. The Behavioral Sciences Unit (BSU) was then officially open for business.* Initially called criminal personality profiling—and referred to as profiling in this book, for simplicity's sake—the deductive reasoning process underwent a number of name changes and eventually became known as criminal investigative analysis.

Violent crime in the US had been steadily increasing since the 1960s and by the mid-1980s had reached alarming proportions. Homicide rates were at an all-time high and investigation solve rates were dropping. The FBI was tasked with helping their government bosses understand the issues and BSU members travelled to prisons across the country undertaking research projects to analyze the workings of the criminal mind. This was groundbreaking research because the questions being asked of violent offenders were from a criminal investigator's perspective rather than an academic's or clinician's. Keeping in mind the propensity for less than accurate responses from criminals, the agents

---

* Over subsequent years the BSU underwent several name changes and reorganizations in accordance with the growing specialized services they provided. For simplicity, I continue to refer to it as the BSU.

always meticulously examined the investigative files of their interviewees before meeting with them.

In one of the first research initiatives, interviewers had face-to-face conversations with sexually motivated killers, adhering to an extensive research protocol developed and analyzed together with doctors internationally recognized for their work in the area. After speaking with thirty-six repeat homicide offenders, the term "serial killer" was coined, that is, the same person committing three or more murders. Further research was conducted over the years in the areas of sexual assault, child sexual abuse and other violent crime issues.

At the same time, on the other side of the country, an LAPD homicide cop was experiencing significant frustration having to time and again go through old newspaper articles and call other area police departments to see if anyone else had similar murders in their jurisdictions. He pitched his idea of a searchable database of violent criminal behaviour and other case information to the United States Department of Justice. It resulted in the establishment of the Violent Crime Apprehension Program (ViCAP), a computerized repository of major violent crime cases submitted by those police agencies that wanted to participate. ViCAP was added to the BSU's profiling, research and consultation programs and, in 1984, President Ronald Regan announced the formation of the NCAVC. Long-time member of the BSU and its first unit chief, Roger Depue was instrumental in getting the police fellowship program off the ground that same year. By the time I arrived in Quantico, Roger had retired, as had most of the other pioneer agents, but I became well acquainted with his and all his agents' work and how they gained their legend statuses when I reviewed their closed-case files. (Roger went on to gather a group of elite retired FBI agent and police fellow profilers, known as the Academy Group, providing parallel international behavioural consulting services to private sector organizations to aid them with a variety of behaviour-based civil and criminal issues.)

What I was about to study, including the BSU's academic research, closed cases and new cases coming in, were some of the most unusual and vicious crimes ever investigated. The graphic details could come in many forms: through written material and photographs, but also via audio and video as the new era of recorded evidence was also emerging. Some days there would be hours of it. I had to be prepared to steel myself for it and manage the stress, to stay detached from the emotion of the open cases being presented, sometimes two or three a day. I learned for my mind and heart to survive and not be haunted by the knowledge and wisdom my teachers imparted, I had to adopt strategies to psychologically disconnect. One was: refer to the "good guys"— the assaulted, the murdered, the survivors by their first names, because the innocent and vulnerable deserved my thoughtfulness. Whereas I would refer to the "bad guys" only by their last names—these perpetrators who were heartless, vicious and cruel and had never exercised restraint or civility in causing human suffering, so I chose to give them no emotional consideration. It was a small thing that somehow helped. But I mostly coped by focusing on my role as a student profiler and concentrating hard on learning from what I was reading, listening to and seeing, and resist getting drawn in to the sensationalism of it all. Keeping my equilibrium was helped a great deal by being anchored with the company of my fellow students and decompressing together at the end of each day. I also took advantage of the state-of-the-art gym that was just a short distance away from my dorm room. On weekends I'd often take my bicycle by car to the outskirts of Washington, and then ride the bike paths into the city and spend the day there. I was eating well, sleeping well, staying fit and became totally immersed in all that I was experiencing.

My FBI training course was definitely not for the faint of heart, including everything from forensics and criminal psychology, to serial rapists and killers, bombers, threat assessment and interrogation tactics. Occasionally I'd be sprung from the bunker, sent for a week-long course in forensic pathology in Bethesda, Maryland, and a forensic psychiatry course in Charlottesville, Virginia. During one memorable week, I travelled to New York City and did a ride-along with the NYPD Crime Scene Unit, which specialized in forensic identification. As luck would have it, actor Robert De Niro was with us that week, conducting research for an upcoming movie. He and I were both assigned to work the night shift with the Bronx Squad.

With 2,262 homicides in the city in 1990, there was not a lot of downtime between calls, but there was much to learn from these officers and the multitude of crime scenes they took us to over the course of the week. Mr. De Niro, always dressed nondescriptly and with a baseball cap pulled down over his eyes, drove to the crime scenes himself in his old rusted-out car. If recognized by bystanders, he'd take off and then meet up with us at the next homicide or other violent crime in the queue. I left

New York with a whole new appreciation of the work done by these NYPD specialists—and, as an added memento, a signed photograph from Mr. De Niro.

Back at the FBI Academy, I particularly enjoyed sitting in on consultations between BSU agents and visiting police officers from all over the world who were searching for new and innovative perspectives on their unsolved violent crime cases. These sessions typically started with a full case overview with all investigative and forensic information. It was not uncommon for the investigators to work in a pitch regarding their personal perspectives and theories about the crime, but you couldn't allow it to impact your own thinking or objectivity. As time went on my observer status slowly changed and I gained the confidence to share my opinions with those around the table. However, on at least one occasion, I may have crossed the line to oversharing.

One time I was participating in an unsolved homicide consultation involving a female victim, and one of my male colleagues voiced his belief that there was a sexual component to the crime because the fully dressed victim had her underpants on inside out. He believed the victim must have at some point during the crime had her underpants taken off and that they were accidentally turned inside out in the process of the offender re-dressing her. From my vantage point I saw no confirmed sexual component in this at all. I had to speak up and confess that on more than one occasion I had discovered that I had come to work with my underpants on inside out. I even admitted to once attending a new assignment interview and not realizing until after it was over that I had been wearing one brown shoe and one black shoe. There were a few snickers but my point was taken.

Crime-scene analysis and reconstruction were grounded in the five Ws: who the victim was, what happened to them, and when, where and why it occurred. It was the last "W," the criminal's motivation, that visiting police were usually having trouble pinning down. Using information provided by ongoing research from the FBI and their partners, we could also explore characteristics of other offenders who had committed similar types of crimes in the past. But when working on a criminal profile there's no such thing as a cookie-cutter approach: individuals and circumstances define the intricacies of each case. Our instructors always emphasized that the profile was a series of opinions, based on the information available at the time the profile was constructed. Investigators needed to keep an open mind and remain objective as they moved through their case and developed further leads and suspects.

Since day one, in addition to his coordinator duties and teaching some of our fellowship classes, Ed Sulzbach was a great ambassador for the State of Virginia, making sure we visited Civil War battle sites, the Blue Ridge Mountains and other attractions. One that Bronwyn and I appreciated discovering was Potomac Mills, one of the largest malls in the country. Sometimes Ed would be out of town for a few weeks working cases, but he'd always hunt us down as soon as he got back, checking in to see how we were doing, and that we had everything we needed. It was always a welcome break from the Academy and its cafeteria food when Ed and his wife, Peggy, invited me and my classmates to dinner at their home in Richmond.

At one of those dinners we were joined by the author Patricia Cornwell, who lived in Richmond. At Ed's suggestion, I bought a copy of her then recently published first book, *Postmortem*, and brought it with me for her to sign. Patsy (as Ed called her) had spent many hours with Ed and others in the BSU, which she said helped in the development of her FBI and police characters for her book. The dedication in her book read, *For Ed, Special Agent and Special Friend*, and I could relate to that sentiment. Not long after, Ed was transferred back to the Richmond FBI field office. I knew he was anxious to get back to fieldwork, but I would miss his guidance and friendship.

STANDING

"The ultimate measure of a man is not where he stands in moments of comfort and convenience, but where he stands at times of challenge and controversy."
—Martin Luther King, Jr.

SUPERVISORY SPECIAL AGENT JUDSON RAY took over as the new fellowship coordinator after Ed left. Judd continued with organizing our course of studies and casework assignments as well as bringing in other members of the unit to give overviews of their work on the high-profile and headline-grabbing atrocities of the day.

Judd's sharing of some of his own tumultuous personal stories was as interesting and educational about life as they were about work. They could be a bit crude, but Judd told them the way they happened. Sometimes they were delivered around the table in the conference room, other times over more than a few cold Samuel Adams beers in "The Boardroom" bar.

Judd grew up in the segregated South of the 1950s. A railway ran through the centre of his hometown of Clayton, North Carolina. The tracks were what separated the blacks from the whites. Judd said, "Whites goes here and coloureds goes there. We knew our place."

There were twelve in Judd's family and they lived off sharecropping. Judd's world changed forever when his mother died when he was thirteen. "Her death started the disintegration of our family. It was a turbulent time for me. I felt like my ability to ever love anything or anybody leaked into that coffin with her."

Judd and his siblings were all separated when sent to live with different relatives in the area. He dropped out of school but later returned and did a short stint in college until he ran out of money after the first semester. He returned home and took a job as a janitor at the local state college campus.

"After about a month, this tall white basketball player came up to me when I was cleaning the athletic dorm. He said he'd been watching me and I shouldn't be cleaning floors and be a janitor for the rest of my life. He told me that I ought to be in college. I knew he wasn't talking about this college because blacks weren't allowed. I told him I had been to the blacks' college but ran out of money."

The student suggested to Judd that he go into the army and they would send him to college. The downside was he would probably have to do a stint in Vietnam. Judd didn't know anything about the army and hadn't even heard of the Vietnam War. "Well I thought it can't be any worse than it is right here." He took the advice to heart and several days later enlisted. It was 1966 and Judd was just nineteen years old.

After basic training Judd was sent to Vietnam for a year. His description of the war's impact on him was surprising to me. "Probably some of the best times of my life were spent in that regiment with those men. It's the first time I ever got a sense of belonging—that there's something, some purpose. There was a lot of discipline there that I probably needed.

"During those years of living on the other side of the tracks I'd seen my share of people dying in the street. A cousin of mine, they called her 'Big Ann,' one night she was shot and killed and she died in my arms. I was only about fourteen. So being in Vietnam, and sounds kind of crazy, but to me the whole idea of dying and death and stuff like that was not a big deal because I had seen it.

"A lot of the other young boys who went over to Vietnam had never even been in a fist fight so it wasn't surprising to me that some of those young ones came back home shattered and had problems with what they saw."

When Judd got back home, he left the army and, in 1968, married a woman whom he had met in the base cafeteria. He had heard Washington, DC, police were looking for officers and was hired right after the riots following the assassination of Martin Luther King.

"I was broken in by an old sergeant. He would have these tidbits of information about how to police. One day we were up on 'I' Street and he says, 'You see those girls there?' I says, 'Yeah.' He says, 'Those are prostitutes.' I says, 'I know what a prostitute is.' He says, 'What you don't know is what I'm gettin' ready to tell ya. Now as a policeman, they have a lot of information.

They're out here. They can be your eyes, ears and they can tell you a lot of stuff. You don't even have to pay them as informers because every now and then you bust one for soliciting and you won't take her to jail and she'll owe you. My point is this. If you're going to work 'em, you can't fuck 'em. If you're going to fuck 'em, you can't work 'em.' That kind of stuck with me about people in general as I kind of came through the policing process.

"You have to declare yourself in terms of what you are and what you stand for and what ditch you're willing to die in. I think Martin Luther King had it right and this is really true with law enforcement. At least it was when I came through. If you haven't figured out that which you're willing to die for, you're not really fit to live. If you don't know what you'd die for . . . it's almost like if you don't know where you stand, you'll sit any-where." Judd hadn't got King's inspirational quote quite right but he surely understood the spirit of it.

Judd also worked for a time with the Columbus Police Department in Georgia. He met BSU agents Roy Hazelwood and John Douglas when they were working together on a serial murder case in Columbus and that eventually led to Judd join-ing the FBI. Several years later John asked Judd if he'd be inter-ested in coming to work in the BSU. Judd jumped at the chance. He was the unit's first black member and one of a very few agents working there with such an extensive violent crime investigation background. He was one of the first in the unit to be qualified as an expert criminal profiling witness in a US court.

By the time I arrived for my fellowship training, Judd was a veteran unit member and one of their top profilers. He was not involved in any major research initiatives, but strictly worked cases. Judd often used his own solved cases to demonstrate the behavioural theories and principles he taught. He always stressed the importance of a methodical crime-scene analysis and a full reconstruction of the events that had occurred in the crime scene before providing any opinion about what had occurred or the type of person likely responsible.

Judd also taught me the concept of crime-scene "staging," that is, the purposeful altering of a scene to misdirect an investigation. The manipulation of a homicide scene to make the death appear to be something else, such as a suicide or an accident, could be indicative of the killer having some type of relationship with the victim. The killer may think he will be a suspect and feel the need to change the scene so that it looks like a motivation other than personal.

Judd usually took out a folder full of photographs and police reports to exhibit a teaching point, but on one occasion all he had with him was a tape recorder. This time, he was neither the investigator nor the profiler for the case study—he was the victim.

It happened after he had finished his FBI new agents training years earlier. He and his wife had just moved to Atlanta with their two young daughters, one eight years old and the other eighteen months. On February 21, 1981, Judd's wife made spaghetti for dinner. After they had finished eating she told him she was going over to her aunt's house with their two kids. "I was feeling a little sleepy after dinner so I lay down. I woke up around ten p.m. and she still wasn't home with the kids so I went to bed. About eleven thirty I wake up hearing a click-click sound. It was right by my head. I come off the bed and somebody bounds out of the bedroom." Judd would find out later that two men had broken into his house. One came into the bedroom and held a gun to his head as he slept. Judd had awakened to the sound of the gun misfiring. This man fled the scene after it happened, but the other remained.

"The next thing a gunshot goes off in the bedroom but it misses me. There's some light coming in the room but I can't make out what the hell is going on. Another shot rings out and hits me in the left arm. Instantly I know that somebody is in here trying to kill me. I guess all of the training kind of floods back. I try to give the guy a very narrow target so I turn sideways on the bed instead of being broadsided.

"Now I know that I've got a situation here. I started talking to the guy. I said, 'Hey man you got the wrong house. What do you want? Just take what you want. I'm not going to give you any reason to kill me.' The guy never says a word. I could see his silhouetted body but I couldn't make out whether the guy is white or black or anything. I realized that I'm hit and I'm talking to the guy and then something goes, 'Man you better be quiet because you may be only directing his fire.' So I shut up and then . . . I'm going, 'This son of a bitch may think that I'm dying so he's going to come in now and finish the job.'

"I start trying to move to the end of this king-size bed. I was thinking, 'This guy is bent on killing me. He wants to get this job done.' My .38 department service revolver is locked up in the bedroom but I can't get to it. And I'm thinking, 'The cops are gonna come in here tomorrow and think this fucking guy never put up a fight about this.' So that was driving me too.

"I started inching my way to the side of the bed and he says, 'Don't move.' So I knew that he knew what my plans were. At least I thought he knew. I kept going and fell off the bed. I'm now facing down on the floor with my right hand caught underneath me. He jumps on the bed and fires one shot, point-blank. The bullet comes through my back, right through my lung, and misses my spine by about an eighth of an inch. The bullet comes out through my chest and through my right hand that was tucked underneath me. I'm bleeding out.

"I remember him putting his damn hands on me like he's checking for a pulse or something. I remember him saying, 'There, motherfucker, die.' Then I hear footsteps walking out of the bedroom.

"I'm lying there hyperventilating because my lung is shot. And I'm pinching myself going, 'Shit I'm dreaming.' I'm thinking I'm doing combat in Vietnam. I never dreamed about Vietnam before. Something was saying, 'Get up, get up, get up.' So I got up and I'm staggering around the room but I can't breathe. Blood is goin' all over the place. So then I lay back at the foot of the bed. I remember thinking I hope this is the last breath because it was getting very, very painful to try to breathe. You can't breathe. I was panicking basically. I lay back down across the bed and I was convinced I was gonna die.

"Then something again said get up and get some water. You don't have to die. So I staggered around walking through my own blood and leaving blood on everything I touched. Finally

I made it into the bathroom. No lights on at all. Turned the faucet on trying to get water and I can't get it. So I pressed the switch to turn the light on. Then I see this fuckin' hand completely splattered, bone sticking up. Now I'm back in touch with reality. I know exactly what happened. I'm bleeding like hell. I know I've got to elevate my hand. I'm in a fix because I can't think how to do this. Plus I think the son of a bitch is still somewhere inside the house. Something says call the police. So I did."

Judd pulled the tape player on the conference room table over in front of him and played the real-time 911 call he made to police that night. He identified himself as an FBI agent to the dispatcher and told her he'd been shot. He was crying and begging them to hurry because he didn't want to die. Judd just stared at the tape player and never looked up. When the call was finished and help arrived, he shut off the tape player and continued the story.

"I passed out for a bit, but remember when the medics arrived, and one of them said, 'This guy ain't gonna make it.' I probably wouldn't have made it if a thoracic surgeon hadn't been walking out of the hospital when they rolled me in on the gurney. He looked over and took his damn scissors out and hit me on the side. Blood flew everywhere because I was drowning. They eventually got me stabilized."

The police put an armed guard outside Judd's room for three weeks until he was released from hospital. His wife and two children were staying with her aunt in Alabama, so he returned home alone.

Judd told us that everyone in his office had quit working on their cases to help police follow up on the multitude of leads coming in. With Judd's police and FBI experience there were a number of potential enemies. He said, "That was at the time that J.R. Ewing got shot on the TV show *Dallas*. I found out later the office joke was, 'Who shot J.R.?' But they were talkin' about me, Judson Ray."

While Judd was recovering at home from his injuries, investigators tried to keep him away from the investigation. But it didn't take Judd to be a profiler to figure this one out: this was personal. There was no doubt in his mind that one person he knew had to be involved—his wife.

One day, shortly after Judd had got home from the hospital, he was catching up on paying his bills. He was going through his telephone bill and noticed that the long-distance portion was high, with numerous calls out of state before the shooting. He knew that his wife must have made the calls. This evidence would put the local police and FBI firmly on the trail of those responsible. Numerous conversations recorded from wiretap authorizations obtained by police sealed the case. Judd's wife and two hired hit men were indicted. Their charges ranged from burglary to attempted murder. All of them got ten years, although Judd's wife was out in three.

Judd related to the class that when he had returned from the FBI's New Agent training in Quantico, he'd known his marriage was over. He'd told his wife he wanted a divorce and custody of their two girls. "I think that started her planning to have me killed. I was worth about quarter-million dollars in insurance.

That probably was one of the real motivators and the fact that I wasn't going to be with her anymore. Looking back, I know she was under a great deal of stress and unhappy in the marriage too.

"Being a victim of a crime, in hindsight, I kind of liken it to a death experience. Oftentimes if you get a bullet in you, you're not around to talk about it. It's almost like I'm having the benefit of having died and to come back to say that this is how it really is. You see how victims can fuck up a crime scene? I contaminated that crime scene walkin' all around, walkin' through my own blood.

"If I had not lived, there's a good possibility that we may have never known what happened because she'd set the apartment up where costume jewellery was stowed around to make it look like an intruder coming in to burglarize the place.

"I'm sure some investigator lookin' at it is thinkin', 'Well this fuckin' guy is marching this guy around trying to find more valuable stuff.' That would be one way of lookin' at this had I not been there to tell exactly what happened. Remember, things don't always happen the way they look."

Judd was right. His death would have looked like he was the victim of a burglary gone wrong. Everyone would have thought he was killed by a stranger breaking into his house.

When Judd was back to work after the shooting, he started to look at other solved cases that were similar to his. He found that the offenders' pre-offence behaviours were often consistent with those of his wife.

"In a close relationship where one of the parties has decided that they're going to kill the other one, I think they behave in ways which may tend to throw cops off. But I don't think it's strategic. In fact, I had a homicide psychologist say he thought it might have more to do with coming to grips with the reality of the decision. Meaning that if you are married and I'm going to hire somebody to kill my spouse, in order for me to become psychologically prepared, I've got to start behaving in certain ways. I've got to kind of behave in ways that convinces me that I've done everything I could for you. I've been as nice as I could to you. That's what my wife was doing at the time. She was paying more attention to me. She would get up and want to know if I wanted breakfast. She never made me breakfast in the thirteen years we were married. I always tell the cops now, 'Look back two or three weeks before this killing if you suspect.' I'm only talking about hired assassin kind of killings. Look back couple or three weeks and see if there's been a change in behaviour."

Judd's wife had set the stage for a crime that she thought she would never be suspected of. And because of that, her actions were not well guarded and came to light during the investigation. She never thought that anyone, least of all her husband, would look through her old long-distance phone bills and put the crime together. Judd had done a methodical reconstruction of his own crime scene and solved it himself.

Typical of Judd, he never strayed far from his sense of humour, saying, "You should get suspicious when your wife all of a sudden starts treating you nice. I loved her spaghetti, but that night, it was laced with phenobarbital."

THE MASTER CLASSES

"Teachers open the doors, but you must enter by yourself."
—Chinese proverb

I FIRST MET SUPERVISORY SPECIAL AGENT Roy Hazelwood late one afternoon when he'd just come back to his office after teaching one of his National Academy courses. I'd heard he'd worked for former BSU chief Roger Depue and helped develop the fellowship program and I wanted to personally thank him for extending the opportunity to Canadians. Roy was sitting behind his desk and wearing a suit, but otherwise was the antithesis of what you'd expect an FBI agent to look like. He was short, slim and wore large eyeglasses. I often saw other BSU members leaving the office at the end of the day carrying athletic bags and taking advantage of a workout at the Academy gym before heading home. Roy didn't look at all like the type that went to the gym at the end of his day. He looked far more likely to shut his office door, open his desk drawer, pour a few shots of something into his coffee cup and chain-smoke more than a few cigarettes until he was ready to call it a day.

Prior to joining the FBI, Roy had worked in the Criminal Investigation Command of the military police. After several years as an FBI agent in the field, he returned to instruct at the Academy in Quantico and eventually took a position in the BSU to do research and teach the "Sex Crimes" course to National Academy students.

When Roy first arrived at his recently vacated basement office, he found that some people with a dubious sense of humour had done some decorating. Bras and panties were hanging on the wall and the desk had a robed statue on it. If you pressed the top of the head, a penis protruded from his frock. Boxes of pornographic magazines and sexual paraphernalia were promptly thrown in the garbage. Roy could see he needed to set a different tone. He renamed the "Sex Crimes" course the "Interpersonal Violence" course to focus on the true seriousness of the crimes.

Roy was one of the main instructors for the academic phase of my training. He made it clear to my class right from day one that no off-colour jokes or stories would be tolerated. He had us watch the 1985 award-winning, groundbreaking and controversial ABC made-for-television movie *Deadly Justice: The Rape of Richard Beck*. Actor Richard Crenna plays the title role of a tough-guy detective who believes that rape victims are at least partly responsible for the crimes committed against them. But when Beck himself is raped and brutalized by two criminals, he undergoes a painful transformation. I could see why it was important to Roy that we view this fictionalized depiction of the mindset of some women and men in a just-ending era of indifference or denial. There was no room for any residue of that stereotypical thinking in Roy's classes.

One of the concepts that Roy taught me that I used in every violent-crime analysis in my career as a criminal profiler involved determining the key aspect in crime scenes of whether they were organized or disorganized. Roy found that some were indicative of preplanning and control, while others seemed more spontaneous and unplanned. He discussed the concept with John Douglas and together they developed from their experiences a list of characteristics, unique to each of the two types of crime scenes.

I used this "lowest common denominator" analytical process when reviewing the solved cases that Roy and other instructors gave me during my training. However, sometimes it appeared that the distinction between the two types of behaviours could not be so easily made. The crime scenes occasionally seemed mixed. Once the review exercise was completed and I was aware of the outcome of the investigation and who was responsible, I went back and tried to determine why the person demonstrated both organized and disorganized features in the same crime scene. In some cases there was a strong possibility that the offender's normal behaviour patterns were altered because of alcohol or drug consumption at the time the crime was committed. Sometimes mixed patterns indicated that there was more than one person involved in committing the crime. In a number of the serial crime cases the offenders may have learned information from the media or even from their previous mistakes, such as one criminal who began wearing gloves after getting convicted of an earlier crime on fingerprint evidence.

It was no surprise that criminal behaviour evolved. To me, it was similar to any law-abiding citizen learning a craft or a trade—you get better at it as you learn on the job.

Roy was also my primary instructor for sexual aggression and all types of adult sexual deviancies. In other types of violent crimes I learned one must understand the mind to understand the crime. With sexually assaultive behaviour I must also understand the sexual fantasies of the perpetrator to understand their motivations and what fuels their crimes.

Roy adapted his typology system for better understanding different types of rapists as first suggested by Nicholas Groth in his book, *Men Who Rape: The Psychology of the Offender*. For the first time I realized this type of interpersonal violence was not motivated solely by sexual aggression, but rather the offender was acting out their power, anger or sadistic nature on their victims. (Two sub-categories for stranger-on-stranger assaults, opportunist and gang related, were later added to these classifications.) The behaviours could range from a stranger sex offender attempting to simulate a consensual relationship with his victim, almost like he was on a date, to the extreme of those that entailed brutally sadistic, degrading and painful sexual and physical assaults causing victims' immense suffering. The verbal, physical and sexual behaviour demonstrated by the attacker during the assaults were the clues to their motivations and sexual fantasies.

I initially found it quite disturbing reading through FBI "solved" files and the statements of surviving victims and the confessions of arrested rapists. Many cases contained photographs, along with audio and videotapes of victims being assaulted and tortured. My intention was never to ignore victims or be insensitive to their mental and physical suffering, but I found it necessary to compartmentalize in my mind those aspects of the crimes. It was a matter of my personal emotional survival if I was to successfully take up this work in the future.

Roy also taught me a process that he helped pioneer known as equivocal death analysis. Police and forensic experts traditionally relied on autopsy results, forensic examinations and other evidence to help determine the cause of a death. However, there were some cases where that didn't necessarily lead to a clear determination of the manner of death or whether even a crime had been committed. This process focused on an analysis to determine whether it was most likely that death resulted from suicide, homicide or by accident. Things were changed up in these types of cases because rather than focus on the behaviours and possible motivations of an offender, the focus was on the deceased. Sometimes referred to as a "psychological autopsy," you had to closely examine all possible clues of what was going on in their personal life in the days, weeks and months prior to their death. All of the deceased's actions and interactions had to be taken into consideration, reconstructed and interpreted before an opinion could be given.

While at Quantico I had an opportunity to review an OPP equivocal death investigation that had been sent to the BSU for a second opinion in 1989. Roy encouraged me to start with a review of the photographs. A man was found deceased inside a one-room shack in northern Ontario. He had died from blood loss due to multiple abdominal stab wounds, five tightly grouped axe wounds to the forehead and castration. His death could clearly have been caused from any of the three types of injuries. It was unbelievable to me to think that the wounds could be self-inflicted and yet the crime scene held another clue. The door and windows of the shack were locked from the inside.

I sought out the opinions of my fellow students and we brainstormed all possible scenarios to reconstruct how this death could have occurred. We even considered staging, but when armed with a full account of this man's personal circumstances, including a family member recently disclosing a sexual assault committed by him, his consumption of a large quantity of alcohol prior to his death and his bloody fingerprint on a liquor bottle, an opinion on the most likely manner of death emerged. We were all confident that the man died of self-inflicted wounds and it was a suicide. Roy had taught us well. The same conclusion was drawn by the FBI analyst back in 1989, as well as the original OPP investigating officer.

Roy brought in BSU member Supervisory Special Agent Ken Lanning, to teach the behavioural aspects of sexual exploitation, abduction, abuse and other crimes related to children. Ken was already recognized as one of the world's leading experts in this field of victimization that he had dedicated his career to since 1973. To say he was passionate about his work was an understatement. I sometimes worried he was going to have a heart attack when he got so agitated discussing topics such as previous generations' denials of the existence of child abuse and the antiquated and inaccurate notion that "stranger danger" was the greatest threat to children's safety.

The reality was that children were very often assaulted by people they knew, including their own family members. These sex offenders did not always physically assault their victims in the traditional or legal sense. They often used their authority, trust, grooming techniques and even seduction. They counted on their victims' responses of confusion, embarrassment, shame and guilt—emotions that prevented them from reporting the abuse or even prompting them to deny it if confronted.

Ken's researched-based theories of the different motivations and types of child sex offenders were documented in his publication "Child Molesters: A Behavioral Analysis."[2] It should be required reading for all involved in the field of sexual victimization of children. When I returned home from Quantico, I never attended a child sexual abuse consultation without having that guide tucked in my briefcase. Ken later included updates on the significant issues created by children and predators having access to the Internet and the use of the Internet for the distribution of child pornography, issues that didn't exist at the time of my training.

Ken also used in his teaching one of the most comprehensive studies of missing children homicides, later published in

"Investigative Case Management for Missing Children Homicides."[3] One of the statistical tables was starkly revealing: for children who had been abducted and subsequently murdered, 47 percent were dead within one hour of the abduction; 76 percent within three hours; 89 percent within twenty-four hours; 98 percent within seven days; and 100 percent within thirty days. It sent a clear message as to why prompt investigative action by police was so critical in such cases. I cited these statistics many times over my career when police were asking for my help in a child abduction case. I also found them useful when trying to persuade my police bosses and provincial government officials to fund initiatives such as a violent crime tracking system, a geographic profiling program and a provincial sex offender registry.

A key fact to keep in mind was that sexually motivated child abductors and killers spent a significant amount of time fantasizing about taking a child and having sex with them. The actual sexual activity was the centre of the fantasy. The abductors spent little time planning the actual abduction or what they would do with the child when they were finished assaulting them. The abduction was often a circumstance of opportunity: a child left alone for a split second by a distracted parent or a youngster walking home from school or from a play date at a friend's house. The killers trolled, waited for the opportunity and when it presented itself, they'd strike.

After the assault was over the offenders were faced with what to do with the child. The child would be panic-stricken, often screaming and crying. They would beg to be let go and promised not to tell their parents—that is, if they were even old enough to talk. Panic would set in for the offenders as well. They often had not thought this part through. Killing was one of their choices. Sometimes they didn't get caught. Sometimes they did.

Those training sessions with Roy and Ken gave me a whole new understanding of sexually assaultive behaviour. Without a doubt it was hardest to work on those cases involving young children as victims, so innocent and vulnerable. I couldn't even fathom what it would be like to be a parent of a child that was harmed or the worst-possible scenario, taken from them and possibly never know what happened to their child.

TAKEN

"To have a child taken . . . is to be struck by lightning out of a clear sky."
—Journalist Bill Cameron in the CBC documentary *Missing*

MICHAEL DUNAHEE—THE FIRST CHILD of Bruce and Crystal—was just a few months away from his fifth birthday. He was a good-natured and outgoing little boy who loved being a big brother to his six-month-old baby sister, Caitlin. On Sunday, March 24, 1991, at 12:30 p.m., Michael was with his family, having just arrived at a school playing field where his mother was to play an afternoon game of touch football. They parked their red Datsun station wagon along the single row of other parked cars on the west side of the playing field. Michael asked if he could go over to the children's playground area at the side of the school. It was a short distance away, just on the other side of an empty basketball court. He was told that he could, but was not to go off playing elsewhere with the other kids on the playground and to stay within sight. It was the first time Michael had ever been allowed to go to a playground alone, but his parents were no more than a hundred metres away and they would be able to easily see him from the football field. Michael went off toward the playground area as his mom was putting on her football cleats and his dad was settling Caitlin into her stroller.

At the football field Bruce checked on the score of the game in progress and then stepped onto a boulder jutting out of the ground at the side of the field so that he could look over top of the cars and keep an eye on his son. Less than a minute had passed since Michael had left his sight. When Bruce looked over toward the playground area, Michael wasn't there. He told Crystal that he was going to go look for him. He searched around the school and between the portable classrooms, calling Michael's name. Bruce ran back to the playing field to tell his wife he couldn't find Michael. Word spread quickly and the football game was stopped. All of the players and spectators fanned out, searching nearby housing complexes, streets and back lanes. A local home owner, outside cutting his lawn, was asked to call the Victoria Police Department.

That afternoon and evening the police and volunteers searched for a little boy who had wandered off. By morning it had turned into a search by over a hundred officers for a little boy who had surely been abducted. Michael, three feet tall, weighing about fifty pounds, blond hair and blue eyes, freckles on his cheeks, and wearing his favourite *Teenage Mutant Ninja Turtles* T-shirt, was never seen again.

Michael Dunahee's disappearance rocked Victoria and the wave of anxiety and anguish it created quickly spread across Canada.

Every major media outlet in Canada and the northwestern US was covering the story. Posters of Michael were distributed across Canada and the US. Bruce and Crystal Dunahee went on television and pleaded for the safe return of their son. They showed numerous photographs of Michael, one holding a stick with two small fish skewered on it that he had caught with his grandpa. In another he was holding his baby sister. They also played video footage of Michael doing his "boogie" dance on his bed as his mother laughed and looked on.

Although Victoria is British Columbia's capital city, it has always had a small-town feel. It was now in the spotlight being talked about, not for its spectacular floral gardens or the magnificent nearby mountains, but for its police department undertaking the largest investigation in Canadian history. Child abductions are thankfully rare; this was the first one to occur in Victoria.

Every parent in Victoria at the time was thinking the same thing—this could have been their child who was snatched while they looked the other way for just a moment. No longer were children allowed to walk to school without some kind of supervision. No longer were they allowed to play outside alone. It was a heartbreaking loss of innocence for the city.

After three weeks of investigation and with no firm or promising leads, Victoria detectives contacted the FBI's BSU for help. As he was responsible for cases that came into the unit from the northwestern parts of the US and Canada, Supervisory Special Agent Steve Etter was assigned as the lead agent on the case.

Steve was just returning to work after a leave of absence and still coming to grips with devastating news of his own. His older daughter, Alexandra, who had been born with a congenital heart defect, had recently died at the age of just two, following surgery. She died on the same day that her new little sister* was born.

A funeral service was held for Alexandra in Dale City, just north of Quantico. The church was packed. Just about all of us from the BSU attended. A photograph of Alexandra was displayed at the front of the church. During the service Steve and his wife, Ellen, holding their baby daughter, came to the pulpit to eulogize Alexandra. They played an audio tape of her singing and chatting. They wanted those of us who did not get a chance to meet Alexandra to get to know who she was. I don't know where they found the strength.

Steve had only been back to work for a few weeks and when I heard he had been assigned a Canadian case, I asked him if I could be involved. It was the first one to come in to the unit from Canada since I'd arrived at Quantico. A few days later I went to pick up the task force investigators from several different BC police agencies at nearby Manassas Regional Airport. They stepped off the private BC government jet loaded down with briefcases, numerous banker's boxes and a gift of two large fresh salmon packed in ice.

The Quantico trip provided the detectives an opportunity to be out of the limelight for a few days. They had not had a day off in weeks. My offer of some relaxation and beverages was eagerly accepted and we left the airport for a nearby tavern. They told me that they were hopeful that the FBI consultation the

* Steve requests that her name be kept private.

next day would bring some new perspectives to their investigation. I let them know we would also be joined by Ken Lanning and gave them an overview of the training I had already received from him.

After a few short hours filled with their sharing what their lives had entailed over the last weeks, the bar owner came to our table and apologized that the tavern was out of beer. I don't think that would ever happen back home in Canada, but I took it as a signal that it was time to leave and get them to their hotel.

The next morning I brought the guys to meet Steve and Ken in one of the small FBI Academy boardrooms on the second floor. They presented all the evidence gathered over the last twenty-nine days in the case and at the end of their presentation there was a good understanding of victimology, the abduction location and neighbourhood demographics. There had been no eyewitnesses. There was no physical evidence. But for the person who took Michael, there had been a high risk of being seen. With virtually no behavioural clues to interpret, there was little information for a crime-scene analysis. The likely personality descriptors of the unknown offender came from the FBI agent's past investigative experiences and the research that Ken and others had conducted into these types of crimes more than anything else. The investigators were reminded that profilers dealt in probabilities, not possibilities. Anything was possible and investigators must keep their minds open to that.

The investigators had explored every lead and were frustrated by the lack of information to move their case forward. They asked the same questions as all dedicated investigators do. Have

92

they missed something? Was there something more they could do? Their time spent in Quantico was also an opportunity for them to stop and take a breath. New eyes had taken a look at their case from a different perspective: eyes that didn't have the media scrutinizing their every move; eyes that didn't have to look at the anguished faces of family members. At the end of our meeting, I was confident that Steve and Ken had given them a better understanding of the most probable type of offender responsible for Michael's disappearance. (As this investigation is still an open, confidential Victoria Police Department cold-case investigation, I can't share any information regarding the details of the consultation, unknown offender profile or investigative suggestions that came out of the meeting.)

When the consultation was finished, lead investigator Detective John Smith thanked all of us for our time and signalled to his team to start packing their charts, reports, notes and photographs back into the banker's boxes.

I saw in their faces and heard in their voices the toll this investigation was taking. Ken Lanning must have noticed it too. He interrupted their task. "Sit back down a minute, guys," Ken said. "Just listen to one more thing I have to say."

"There will come a time when this case will end for you," Ken began. "All leads will have been followed up and in the end the person responsible for what happened to Michael Dunahee may never be found. Michael may never be found." The room was silent.

"If that is what happens, you are still great police officers who did a great job. You are doing everything you can to solve this case. You will never let down the public, the Dunahee family or Michael. Remember that. Please."

A few days later I went with the officers to the Washington studio filming of an *America's Most Wanted* television episode featuring a segment on Michael Dunahee. The show's host, John Walsh, was well known as a victims' advocate since the murder of his own child, Adam, in 1981. The popular reality show first aired in 1988 and had helped to bring numerous missing children home. Detective Smith was featured on the syndicated show and dozens of tips were called in. The show rebroadcast parts of Michael's story with updates on five separate occasions and later a $100,000 reward for information was offered but no tips received have resulted in any substantiated leads.

Michael Dunahee, age 4   Michael age-enhanced to 26

MIND HUNTING

"To understand the artist you must look at the artwork . . . to understand the criminal you must look at and study the crime itself."
—John Douglas

FROM MY DAY-TO-DAY INTERACTIONS in the BSU I could see the pressure that the agents were under working all these high-profile and stressful cases. They were assigned a huge caseload and were continually travelling around the country and internationally to do on-site consultations. Many were also teaching Academy courses, as well as presenting at various FBI "field schools," seminars and conferences, that again required them to be away from their office caseloads.

A number of BSU members were off on sick leave when I first arrived. Others had been afflicted in the past with serious illnesses undoubtedly related to the stress of working in such an environment. Even the recently promoted BSU chief, John Edward Douglas, had in the past contracted such an illness—and it almost cost him his life.

When I first met John, I thought he epitomized what an FBI agent would look like. He was tall, fit, good-looking and well-dressed, down to the monogrammed "JED" shirt cuffs. I had heard rumours about his large ego and that he even joked about it. But the first day John spoke to my class he was all business and cautioned us about the mental and physical toll that the work could take. We knew he spoke to us from experience.

In December 1983, at thirty-eight years of age, John suffered a near-fatal brain hemorrhage from viral encephalitis. He was working on numerous high-profile serial murder cases, travelling to different parts of the US and Canada to do on-site consultations. He was also trying to keep up with a full schedule of speaking engagements. He acknowledged that he was extremely fatigued, working too much, drinking too much, having trouble sleeping, and overall under tremendous stress. He was in Seattle, Washington, when he started to feel physically ill and thought he was getting the flu. Two colleagues later found him collapsed in his hotel room and called for an ambulance. John was in critical condition when he arrived at the hospital and slipped into a coma. A week later he came out of the coma with stroke-like physical impairments, including partial paralysis. It took him five months of gruelling rehabilitation therapy before he achieved a full recovery. Unfortunately, when he returned to work John found out that nothing much had changed in relation to the workload assigned to BSU staff. He told us that he hoped that our class, especially those of us from outside the US, would return to our departments and help with the BSU workload in the future.

I was acquainted with most of the officers that John had worked with in Canada and he had a reputation for seeming to put aside whatever he was working on with an "if you need me, I'll be there" attitude. He and other unit members had been travelling to Toronto to provide their crime-analysis services for almost a decade. The head of the city's specialized investigative squads was a National Academy graduate and familiar with the BSU's services. All were high-profile cases: the murder of a Welsh nanny, Christine Prince, who was abducted while walking home after an evening out with friends (a case that remains unsolved); a re-investigation of the deaths of children being treated on the cardiac ward at the Hospital for Sick Children (no longer classified as homicides); the murder of University of Toronto student Deliana Heng (solved through DNA match and conviction of Tien Poh Shu); the murder of eleven-year-old Alison Parrott (solved with DNA match and conviction of Francis Carl Roy): and a series of seven unsolved sexual assaults in the Toronto suburb of Scarborough.

When John found out I was working in Toronto, he was eager to talk about one case in particular that he had been involved in. In 1984 Toronto officers introduced John to the Durham Regional Police detectives investigating the abduction and murder of nine-year-old Christine Jessop in Queensville, about an hour north of Toronto. John went with investigators to the area where the young girl lived and was last seen, as well as the location where her body was discovered three months after she went missing. The next morning he provided the officers with a tape-recorded "unknown offender profile." After he had done that, John was told that Christine's twenty-three-year-old neighbour, Guy Paul Morin, was a suspect. John listened to a taped interview of him and agreed with the investigators that he seemed to be a good suspect. Some of the characteristics and traits that John believed the killer would possess matched the neighbour, others did not. They discussed investigative strategies, including releasing parts of his profile to the media and observing how this neighbour reacted before they interviewed him again.

I was already familiar with this case because there was so much media attention given not only to Christine's murder, but also because Morin had since been arrested, charged and then acquitted at his 1986 trial. John was adamant in standing behind his original unknown offender profile of the still-unidentified killer.

(The case didn't end there. It was appealed and retried twice, finally ending in Morin being acquitted of Christine's murder, released from his life imprisonment sentence and receiving a $1.25 million settlement. A later public inquiry provided 119 recommendations, three of which related to the use of criminal profiling services by police, all of which I agreed with and supported: that police be aware of the limitations of profiling; that profiles must not be modified by police after the fact and inappropriately disseminated to the public; and that information provided to profilers should be in writing.)

After three decades Christine's murder remains unresolved.

———

John's unit occasionally shared some of the violent and graphic details of the cases brought to them by investigators with visiting authors and others in the media. Some were even allowed to sit in on training sessions given by members of the BSU at the FBI Academy. One of the first was bestselling author Thomas Harris, whose book, *The Silence of the Lambs*, featured a dramatized depiction of the work done in the unit. The movie version, partly filmed at the FBI Academy, was released in January 1991 while I was attending my training. It was a box office hit that brought international interest to the real-life work being done in the BSU.

The movie was not a particularly accurate portrayal of the real work done by FBI profilers—for instance, selecting a rookie agent to assist in the investigation of a serial killer would just never happen. However the Academy phones rang for weeks after the movie's release as thousands of young people called to get information on how to become an FBI profiler. Distractions were intense in the unit as a multitude of media, such as Lesley Stahl's *60 Minutes* TV crew, were given access to interview John and other agent profilers, as well as film inside the unit. At first it was all quite exciting for me as a visiting police fellow, but it was brought to an end when it became too disruptive to the office.

On July 25, 1991, my training assignment with the FBI was officially over when the police fellows' graduation ceremony and banquet was held at the Quantico Marine Base officers' mess. John and most of the members in the unit involved in our training attended. It was a proud time for all of us, and especially moving to have our families there with us. OPP commissioner

Tom O'Grady flew in earlier in the day to attend the event. As a former National Academy graduate, he had used his contacts in the FBI to obtain the OPP's police fellowship position. We got sad news just before dinner when the commissioner received word that forty-one-year-old OPP sergeant Thomas Cooper had just been shot and killed while responding to a firearms complaint. This was announced to the banquet attendees and a moment of silence followed. The commissioner and I were very touched by this expression of respect and solidarity.

Early the next morning, I drove the commissioner back to the airport as he was anxious to get home to Ontario to meet with the slain officer's family. I returned to the Academy to finish packing, say my goodbyes and drive with Bob and my family in a convoy back to Canada. I was anxious to get my personal life off hold and particularly wanted to get home to plan my wedding as Bob had proposed on a weekend that he'd visited me at Quantico. It had taken me thirty-five years to find the person I wanted to spend the rest of my life with and I wanted to get living it.

The BSU had its office politics and its various egos, sometimes at odds with one another, but I can't say that I ever worked in a high-stakes office environment that was exempt from that. I didn't care who interviewed which infamous serial killer, who coined which profiling term, who was working on the most high-profile case, or even who in the office the character Jack Crawford in *The Silence of the Lambs* movie was fashioned after. I did my best to stay out of the politics while I was there and soak up as much as I possibly could.

There is a Japanese proverb that goes something like, "Knowledge without wisdom is a load of books on the back of an ass." I was leaving Quantico feeling like I was riding a thoroughbred racehorse. I had been provided massive amounts of specialized knowledge but that was only half of it. I had just spent the last ten months of my life working with these agents and my fellowship colleagues on unsolved major criminal investigations from around the world. The FBI had given me the opportunity to be involved in the investigation of crimes that had more peculiar, deviant, cruel and bizarre behaviours than I ever could have imagined a human being would be capable of. The cases didn't always get solved, but every analysis gave investigators, and me, a new perspective, insight and confidence in our abilities.

I will always be grateful to Roger Depue for creating this educational opportunity for police officers and to John Douglas and his agents for the knowledge and wisdom they shared with me when I attended their training program. As it turned out, mine was the last class the FBI hosted, citing budget cutbacks as the reason. But the academic education and practical experience that I was given was second to none that I received over the rest of my thirty-three-year policing career. And there was a lasting bonus: it yielded me lifelong friendships with my fellow trainees and many of the FBI agents and others that I met at the Academy. When I graduated the program, I had the wherewithal to return to Canada and hang out my shingle as a criminal profiler in a time when few had even heard of criminal profiling. I was exhilarated and admittedly a bit nervous. But I knew that all of my FBI mentors and colleagues were only a phone call away. Also, recent graduate Ron MacKay and I had been in touch with one another throughout my course and he assured me that since he was living in Ottawa he was only a few hours' drive away whenever I wanted his help.

OPEN FOR BUSINESS

*"Confidence comes not from always being right but
from not fearing to be wrong."*
—Peter T. McIntyre

WHEN I GOT BACK FROM QUANTICO, I was transferred to
work at Criminal Investigation Branch (CIB) located on the third
floor of OPP headquarters in downtown Toronto. The detective
inspectors (DIs) assigned to the elite branch were the best-of-the-
best detectives, responsible for investigating all major crimes such
as homicides, and also assisted in extraditions, coroner's inquests,
judicial inquiries and any other of our serious criminal investigations or those of other police services who requested their help.

Rather than the bullpen office setting I'd always worked in
before, everyone here had their own offices. As a corporal I was
lower in rank than the dozen or so DIs but was given a large corner office since the guys were usually on the road working their
cases and didn't use theirs much. Once again I was working out
of a vacant boardroom, but it was nice not to have to share it with

six other people. Unfortunately fresh air wasn't abundant in this workspace either because if I'd even been able to get my window open, I'd have been close enough to feel the wind of six lanes of traffic whizzing by on the Gardiner Expressway, which runs across the south end of the city. But for the first time I had my own office, which allowed me to hang my FBI graduation certificate and signed De Niro photograph on a "me" wall. It was all I had to potentially impress my co-workers compared to the multitude of certificates and "attaboy" plaques hanging in their offices.

There were a couple of DIs whom I knew previously from when I was undercover or working frauds and they showed me the office ropes, but I got off to a slow start in my profiling business. I soon realized that an old boys' club largely prevailed. The guys were a friendly enough bunch but offers to go for coffee, lunch, after-work drinks, or even to take a look at one of their unsolved cases were few and far between, at least initially.

I had a great deal of respect for the DIs and was confident that their dedication to do everything they possibly could to solve their cases would eventually outweigh their possible skepticism of the new "hocus-pocus" criminal profiler, and a woman at that. There were some dinosaurs with reputations for sticking solely to traditional methods of investigation, but eventually most of them came knocking on my door seeking input on their unsolved cases. I was happy when any of them did, even knowing that they likely were acting out of desperation or because the boss told them to. I know that at least one DI never did divulge to his co-workers that he had come to me to have a look at his unsolved homicide case and share my thoughts on it.

I wasn't in the profiling saddle too long when I got a chance to compete for a DI position in CIB and was successful. Word got back to me that some of the guys were worried that because I was now a commissioned officer I would want to buy a "CIB ring" to signify my promotion to their rank. I was told wearing the ring was a very big deal to these guys and that, unofficially, the right to wear one was reserved for only those DIs that got a murder conviction in one of their cases. I thanked my insider for the whisper in my ear and at the next staff meeting set the guys straight that the only jewellery I was interested in having on my finger was a wedding ring. I also took the opportunity to bring up an issue of my own.

I'd been given a pager when I arrived in CIB and all the pager numbers in the office were sequential. I was getting regular late-night pages by a sultry-voiced young woman leaving messages about what a great time she'd had that evening. Given the commentary on body parts that obviously had nothing to do with me, the messages were clearly meant for one of my colleagues. She never left a number so I couldn't call her back and set her straight. In the meeting I told the guys that I was proud to work in CIB, and particularly proud of the "work" of whomever these pages were intended for, but asked that they please ensure in future that they give out their correct pager number. The boys had a laugh, the pages stopped and from that moment on the boys seemed to accept me into their fold, even without the ring.

The eventual success of my burgeoning profiling business hinged on the overt support of my CIB colleagues and senior detectives from other police agencies, particularly the Toronto Police Service, which had been using the services of FBI profilers for years. Being asked to speak at their seminars and conferences was a great asset in introducing me and my services to police across Ontario. It also helped when my involvement in their cases was mentioned in the media.

After the release of *The Silence of the Lambs* movie and its five Academy Award wins, there was overwhelming public interest in criminal profilers and a television and movie industry anxious to exploit the interest and excitement. Since I was one of only two profilers in Canada, there were a significant number of media requests for interviews and to appear on radio and TV talk shows. It was all good for my business and my ego until I got burned on an arson case—if you'll pardon my choice of words.

A serial arsonist targeting vacant and abandoned commercial buildings was on the loose and the fires were increasing in frequency as was the likelihood of someone soon getting hurt or worse. I got a call from a local newspaper reporter and was asked to comment on the investigation. I made it clear that I was not involved in the investigation but thought making some general comments on arsonist behaviours would be okay. I was wrong. The next morning the newspaper ran the story as though I had been commenting directly on the case, what the arsonist's motive was and what his profile characteristics would be. I knew the investigators would be really annoyed and rightfully so. I called the detective in charge right away and apologized for my naiveté and said I hoped my comments had not been detrimental to his investigation. He was good about it, said the reporter was a "slime" and told me not to worry about it. My next call was to the journalist to share my displeasure. He couldn't have cared less. Lesson learned.

Ron MacKay, my fellow Canadian profiler, drove down from Ottawa to meet with me shortly after I got back from Quantico.

I liked his "tell it like it is" style and he and I became fast friends. Other than our both being in the same business and sharing a fondness for a cold Molson Canadian, we had little in common. There was truly a generation of difference between us. I was just five years old when Ron joined the RCMP in 1961. He was from Saskatchewan and all of his police postings were in British Columbia until he got the Ottawa profiling position. Most of his career had been spent working on violent crimes, including an investigative review of the 1985 Air India bombing.

In the early days we worked on almost all of our cases together. Ron always opted to look at the crime-scene photographs first and I preferred to hear or read about who the victim was and the details of the crime first and then go through the photographs. Ron would methodically work through the details of a case in chronological order, whereas I was more comfortable working backwards from the commission of the crime. Ron and I would independently reach the same conclusions in different ways, and sometimes for different reasons, which boosted our confidence in the opinions we were providing to police. We agreed that we made great partners.

I knew I would want Ron's assistance when I was asked to do an equivocal death analysis on a case brought to me by CIB DI Mike Coughlin. Mike and I had worked together in Anti-Rackets Branch and knew each other well. His case concerned the death of a young male university student initially found unconscious at the bottom of a dormitory stairwell. It appeared he had fallen from the uppermost level of the staircase. He died a short time later in hospital from severe head injuries. Mike told me the teen was the nephew of a retired OPP officer, John, a former colleague who I was still friends with.

John and his family felt strongly that the death was a homicide. They were devastated not only by their loss but also by the decision of the local police to close the investigation with a finding of suicide. The OPP had been brought in for a coroner's inquest, a legal inquiry into the medical cause and circumstances of a death.

I reviewed all the case material and prepared a preliminary analysis and opinion. Ron and I were going to a serial murder conference in Windsor the following weekend to co-present with our FBI instructor, Roy Hazelwood, so it was a timely opportunity for me to bring both Ron and Roy in on the case too and get a triple check of my opinion. Since I knew John, I also wanted to make sure my analysis would not appear to be biased. Mike came to Windsor as well and we all met in Roy's hotel room one night for more than six hours going over the file material. At the end of the consultation we all had the same opinion as to the manner of death.

Given Roy's pre-existing court-qualified expertise and credibility, it was agreed that he should be the behavioural expert witness to present the equivocal death analysis results at the inquest. Roy returned to Canada a few weeks later, and Ron, Roy and I holed up again in a hotel room, this time for three days, preparing Roy for his inquest testimony. We painstakingly reviewed every detail in the four-hundred-page case file, including police and forensic reports, photographs and witness statements from family, friends and fellow students at the university regarding the young man's behaviour prior to his death.

No one residing in the area of the stairwell heard anything unusual the night of the incident. The student was described by some to be a loner, introverted, moody and with few close friends. There was information that he had been bullied and harassed by several students. He seemed to have had an interest in another female student, but nothing had come of it. His grades had been steadily dropping and he had recently lost a scholarship.

The police also had forensic evidence from the stairwell: the glasses worn by the deceased. They were found upside down on the top-floor landing as if they had been set there. The lenses were not scratched as you might expect if they had accidentally fallen onto the concrete floor during a struggle. The three of us considered not only this and other evidence found at the scene, but also what was absent. That is, in order to be firm in our opinion as to the manner of death, we also undertook to disprove the other possible manners of death, including the possibility of staging. We listed each piece of information and evidence that we had that was and wasn't consistent with a possible manner of death. We even went to the university site so that we could see the scene for ourselves.

Roy was convinced that the time we spent preparing him to take the stand, which he estimated at collectively about 150 hours, was far better than being less prepared and spending those same hours answering questions in the stand. He was right. On the stand, Roy gave a thorough and complete overview of his analysis and findings in just three hours. It was the first time such an analysis was presented in a civil court proceeding in Canada. John represented his nephew's family in the proceedings and had only a few questions for Roy.

When I came into the inquest room to watch Roy testify, I saw and spoke to John only briefly. By that time he was aware of my involvement in helping to prepare Roy to be a witness. We said hello, I expressed my condolences, he accepted them and that was it. It was uncomfortable to say the least.

In the end, the five-person jury found that the manner of death was consistent with ours and that the young man had taken his own life. Sadly, John and I never spoke again.

NOT AN ENEMY IN THE WORLD

"Crime is terribly revealing. Try and vary your methods as you will, your tastes, your habits, your attitude of mind, and your soul is revealed by your actions."
—Agatha Christie, *And Then There Were None*

IN APRIL 1992 I RECEIVED A CALL from DI Jim Hutchinson asking for my help with a homicide case he was working in Caledon. Hutch and I had known one another for a number of years, having met when I did some undercover projects for him when he was a corporal in the London Drug Enforcement Section. When I'd first got back from Quantico, Hutch and I had chatted in the office about my training and the types of cases that were appropriate for "unknown offender profiling." He was anxious for me to take a look at this case as soon as I could. Hutch was working it jointly with the Toronto Homicide Squad, and asked that I meet him the next day at the scene of the crime.

———

An hour's drive north of Toronto, Caledon is a predominantly rural area, boasting beautiful lakeside homes, sprawling country estates and quaint hobby farms. The property owned by Ian and Nancy Blackburn was just off a main regional highway on a quiet side road with farm fields and pockets of forests all around.

The Blackburns owned an upscale home on a quiet residential street in downtown Toronto, but their Caledon property consisted of a small unpretentious white clapboard house built overtop an original log building with a wraparound porch. It was tucked in a short distance from the road amongst a small grove of maple, elm and pine trees and an adjacent apple orchard. An unusual octagon-shaped barn, built in 1890, was situated a few hundred metres atop a small knoll overlooking the farmhouse. There was no grand gated entrance with electronic entry at this farm property, just a simple wooden gate secured with a length of chain and a padlock.

Ian Blackburn's sister, Susan, and her husband, Orville Osbourne, also owned a home in Toronto as well as the property next door in Caledon. These two fifty-acre properties were willed to them by their father so they and their families could enjoy their own weekend retreats.

The Blackburns and Osbournes had heard media reports in recent weeks regarding area homes, vacant during the winter, being broken into. A variety of items had been taken, such as clothing, shoes, jewellery and coins. Long arms and handguns had also been stolen from a residence just south of their farms. It appeared that the person responsible for these break and enters squatted at the properties for some time as well. He became known as the "House Hermit."

Some pornographic magazines were left behind in these residences, as well as some other evidence that was very strange—packages of human feces wrapped neatly in paper or plastic bags, and urine collected in large plastic juice bottles. Most of the locations didn't have any indoor plumbing operating in the winter but keeping the human waste over a period of time was at the very least bizarre behaviour. There were also pages and pages of what appeared to be lists of wartime planes, naval ships, submarines and weaponry, all written out by hand.

On one occasion a couple checking on their cottage were confronted at gunpoint by a man and forced to drive him to Toronto. During the drive to the city the man told them he was wanted on outstanding fraud charges. He wanted them to take him to their Toronto residence, but at a busy downtown intersection the husband stopped the car abruptly, told him to get out and he fled.

A few weeks later another vacation home was being checked by some friends of the owner. They were initially confronted at gunpoint by a man who then fled. He was similar in description to the man in the kidnapping case.

On Tuesday, April 7, 1992, Ian Blackburn, fifty-four, decided to take some time off from his real estate business and drive up to spend the day at his farm. Ian was not seen at the farm, but several area residents, including his sister, brother-in-law and a patrolling OPP officer, did see his Cadillac parked in the farmhouse lane that day.

Nancy Blackburn, forty-nine, was a public health nurse who

often worked at Toronto-area schools and volunteered at a homeless shelter. The Blackburns didn't have any children. They rarely frequented their farmhouse in the winter as Nancy suffered from lupus, which made it difficult for her to be at the farm in the colder weather. But every spring Nancy braved the weather to attend Ian's family's annual "sugaring off" party to enjoy the maple syrup made from their shared maple bush. It was not uncommon for Ian to come up early and check on the property and get it ready for Nancy's arrival.

Later that afternoon back in Toronto, Nancy came home from work and was surprised Ian wasn't yet home. She called some friends, trying to locate him, and expressed concern. Police would later retrieve telephone information that a three-minute call was made at 7:36 p.m. that night from the Blackburns' farmhouse in Caledon to their Toronto home. Nancy did not show up to work the next day.

The Osbournes had a key to the Blackburns' farmhouse and, when they didn't see or hear from either of them for several days, they went in to have a look around. They found nothing amiss. There were two garment bags neatly placed on the bed in the downstairs bedroom. When Ian and Nancy didn't attend the annual party on the weekend, the Osbournes contacted other relatives, friends and co-workers wondering if any had seen or heard from Ian or Nancy. No one had.

On Monday, April 13, the Osbournes called their son back in Toronto and he went to the Blackburns' home to see if there was any sign of them or anything inside the house that would indicate where they'd gone. Nancy's Chevrolet was parked in the driveway. Mail and newspapers were piled up outside the front door. Inside, everything seemed normal except he noticed his aunt's purse was left open on her bed. He called his father to report back. Orville Osbourne then called the local OPP detachment to report Ian and Nancy missing.

At his father's request the young man returned again that evening to see if the Blackburns' cat was in the residence. It was thought that if their cat was still there then they hadn't anticipated being away long. When he re-entered the home he found the cat in the basement. It apparently hadn't been tended to for some time as it had no water or food in its bowls. He then decided to check inside his aunt's car parked in the driveway with a spare set of keys he found. He noticed there was a tissue on the front seat that appeared to have blood on it. When he went on to check the trunk, he made a horrific discovery: Ian's and Nancy's bodies were inside.

Finding out the couple had been reported missing in Caledon, CIB was contacted by Toronto and Hutch assigned. By the time Hutch called me the initial forty-eight hours had come and gone and he was convinced he had a whodunit on his hands. Family members and friends had been cleared of any suspicion. No persons of interest in the investigation had been identified.

One of the advantages of being an OPP rather than FBI profiler was that many of my cases allowed me the ability to travel to the crime scene while it was still being held under authority of a search warrant. That was rarely possible for the FBI given the geographic area they covered and the size of their caseloads. It was important that I wait until all forensic-scene examinations were completed so that I didn't contaminate the scene or evidence in any way. TV shows portraying profilers walking through crime scenes and picking up evidence to take a closer look are far from reality. Try walking into a real crime scene being processed by a forensic identification team (Ident) taking photographs and seizing evidence, and you'd get escorted out by the scruff of the neck.

Reviewing crime-scene photographs was a vital step in the process of crime-scene analysis and reconstruction, but the ability to see everything firsthand was the best. I also always took the time to have a look around the area to get a sense of the community in which the crime occurred. In this case, I drove up to Caledon early so that I could drive around the side roads and into some of the local towns.

Hutch was waiting for me at the farmhouse when I arrived and first showed me around back of the house where it appeared a window had been pried open with some type of tool like a screwdriver. Since the farmhouse had already been processed by the Ident, we were able to go through it together. Inside Hutch pointed out the window in the bedroom which was the possible entry point of an offender. He also showed me where the Ident had located some tiny smears of blood at the top of a set of stairs leading to a loft area and in the dining room area on a trap door leading down to the basement.

Although any forensic evidence was obviously important, my primary interest was being able to observe any indications of behaviour that occurred within the scene. In this case, what drew most of my attention was what I wasn't seeing. The inside of the house didn't indicate any type of altercation or commotion. There wasn't any furniture knocked over or broken that would be consistent with a struggle. Everything was neat and tidy. Everything seemed to be in its place. Except for the two minute areas of blood on the floor, there was no evidence of any potential violence. Hutch and I went back outside and walked around the property and even took a look inside the eight-sided barn. There was nothing out of the ordinary there either.

Hutch was working closely with Doug Grady of the Toronto Homicide Squad. Hutch and I met with that team on the following Sunday afternoon at the Blackburns' Toronto home. Again, there was no evidence of any significant altercation or violence inside this neat and tidy residence either. Although Nancy's vehicle had already been removed from the scene for examination, I inquired as to the setting of the driver's seat, thinking this would give an indication of the stature of the last driver. Apparently the seat had been positioned farther back than what would be consistent with Nancy's stature.

I knew there wouldn't be anyone in my office on a Sunday evening so I went there and just sat at my desk thinking and trying to reconstruct in my mind the various scenarios that could have occurred. Ian and Nancy were married for almost twenty-five years and were described as a loving and devoted couple with not an enemy in the world. Their two homes were located in low-crime areas. They didn't appear to have anything in their background or in their current lifestyle that escalated their risk of becoming victims of a violent crime. They had many friends and no known enemies. The only peripheral issue affecting their susceptibility to becoming victims was the recent criminal activity in the surrounding area where the man had been breaking into unoccupied homes. There was also the one occasion where possibly the same guy had kidnapped the two victims and he'd had a handgun. This could not be ignored, but otherwise the Blackburns were low-risk victims.

It was impossible to know with any certainty where the Blackburns first encountered their killer. Although I didn't know who made the phone call to Toronto from the farm, it seemed most likely that Nancy was summoned to the farm and drove up on her own. Unlike in TV shows, there are information gaps in these types of cases and reconstruction efforts will lack clarity in some areas. There was a lot of blurriness in this one, but what was most important to me was that Ian went up alone, and Nancy for some unknown reason was brought up to join him. The bad guy must have wanted her there. It seemed this crime had more to do about Nancy than Ian. The test results from the two blood-droplet samples from the house hadn't come back yet. It was just a hunch but I was betting the blood would be Nancy's. I picked up the phone and called Ron at home. I wanted our two minds on this one. He said he needed to wrap up a couple of things he was working on but would be down from Ottawa as soon as he could. Some profilers preferred to go it alone with their cases but I always preferred, when possible, to consult with Ron or other experienced officers who could bring different perspectives and challenge my opinions.

———

Two days later Ron and I sat down with Ron Gentle, who'd been assigned to assist Hutch with the case. He had the photographs from the Blackburns' two residences and their autopsies. He also had a copy of the forensic pathologist's report, including the findings and comments. As was our custom, I reviewed the reports as Ron MacKay went through the photos. Then we exchanged them. Over the next few hours our unknown-offender profile emerged.

Nancy's nude body was located farthest inside the trunk of her car. The autopsy report noted she had a small cut in her scalp over her left ear which could be expected to have produced at least some blood. There appeared to be blunt-force injuries and significant bruising all over her body. Ligature marks were found on her ankles, wrists, neck and mouth. The latter was consistent with a gag. The ligature on her neck likely caused petechial hemorrhages in her eyelids and eyes resulting from ruptured capillaries.

When Nancy's body was examined internally the pathologist found deep bruising in her shoulder joints. In his opinion, her hands and feet had been bound together behind her back and then tied together. With Nancy's fragile health, such tight bindings, obviously applied while she was alive, would have been very painful. There was no forensic indication that Nancy had been sexually assaulted, however, this didn't necessarily mean that an assault hadn't occurred, as women who are attacked and vaginally penetrated do not always present with a detectable injury. The pathologist's opinion as to the cause of Nancy's death was asphyxia by ligature strangulation.

Ian was fully clothed and during his autopsy his wallet was found in the back pocket of his pants. Similar to his wife's wallet found in their Toronto home, it contained his personal identification and credit cards but no cash. Ian had a blunt-force injury on his neck and ligature marks on his right wrist, over his thighs and above the knees. He too had petechial hemorrhages in his eyelids and eyes resulting from ruptured capillaries and indicative of asphyxia. There was dried blood around his nose and bruising on his lower lip consistent with a blow or contact with a hard surface. There was a cluster of round symmetrical bruises on the right side of Ian's face. It looked like his face had been repeatedly "stamped" with considerable force. The pathologist's opinion was that the shape and size of these bruises was consistent with the muzzle of a gun. The pathologist's opinion as to the cause of Ian's death was asphyxia, but the possibility of ligature or manual strangulation or even a bag being placed over his head was a possibility.

Given the post-mortem lividity (settling of the blood in the tissues of the body after death) in their bodies, it was the doctor's opinion that both had been placed in the trunk of the car after they died. Neither their ligatures nor Nancy's clothing were found in the trunk of the vehicle or anywhere at the farmhouse or their Toronto home.

Given Nancy's health, her injuries and the bindings applied, the pain she suffered would have been more than that of her husband. The forensic testing results of the minute droplets of blood from the farmhouse in Caledon were now known to be consistent with Nancy's blood. That indicated Nancy was in the farmhouse at some point and her scalp injury likely caused the blood droplets.

In consideration of all of this information, Nancy was the primary victim. The main motive for the crimes was sexual and they would have been committed by a male offender. He appeared to be acting out a sexually sadistic fantasy and demonstrated a seeming rage against Nancy.

Most crimes are intraracial in nature and there was no indication that the offender would be anything other than white.

Age is never an easy opinion to give because the behaviour a criminal exhibits tends to be based more on emotional and mental maturity rather than chronological age. Crimes of interpersonal violence are usually committed by someone in the same age range as the victims. In this case it was lowered to thirty-five to forty-five years of age because of the physical requirements of some parts of the crimes, such as placing the bodies in the trunk of a car. If he was outside that range, he would be older rather than younger given the maturity of the overall crime—meaning that it was well executed and there was very little physical evidence left behind. Also, there was nothing indicative of a second person being involved in this crime.

The scenes in Caledon and Toronto reflected an offender who had immediate control of his victims. He was patient with whatever ruse was used to get Nancy to come to the farmhouse. He was neat and left little evidence behind, seemingly cautious and a planner. He was definitely what is described as an organized offender.

The farm was remote and isolated but the Caledon area would be in this guy's comfort zone. He was knowledgeable and comfortable enough to find and stay in the Blackburns' home for some time, so he may have known them or known of them.

They may or may not have known him. There would be some connection between them but one could only speculate what it might be.

With the bruising pattern on Ian's right cheek consistent with the muzzle of a gun, a firearm was the way the offender controlled his victims.

Given the whole way this crime went down, along with our training and knowledge of FBI and other research into similar cases, Ron MacKay and I agreed that it seemed this offender would likely be asocial but functional and that other traits consistent with this personality would follow. He could be uncomfortable around people but would interact when necessary or in his best interest. He would be seen by others as quiet and reserved and likely seen by some as an eccentric. He probably had a poor self-image. His personal hygiene and the way he dressed would be average to below average. He seemed the type that would work with his hands but was likely unemployed at the time. He certainly didn't appear to be commuting anywhere to work. He would have a criminal record, but likely only for minor offences like this break and enter.

This guy had the time to plan, develop and execute this crime and he didn't appear to be accountable to anyone else. Therefore, he was likely single at the time, although he may have been married in the past. If he was married, his wife would have been considered by him to be inferior to him either mentally or physically. She was likely to be more of a mother figure than a wife.

He must have been very determined in his intentions, because he significantly raised his risk of being caught when he took Ian

KATE LINES

and Nancy to Toronto. He didn't use his own car so perhaps he didn't own one. If he did own one, it would just have been basic transportation, nothing flashy. It seemed more likely that he didn't own a car and maybe didn't even have a driver's licence.

Ron MacKay and I agreed that sexual sadism seemed the strongest component in this crime. Roy Hazelwood had taught us both about sexually sadistic crimes and we were seeing that behaviour in the injuries to Nancy. We also had the knowledge of research conducted by the FBI and others into hundreds of these types of crimes and the men responsible for committing them. These attackers performed degrading acts on their victims that caused pain, suffering and humiliation. There would also have been psychological pain, not only for Nancy but also for Ian if he was present. What was so aberrant about it was that it was sexually arousing to the offender.

The first big break in the case came when searchers located a bag of garbage in a ditch about a hundred metres away from the farm. Inside was an empty can of beer, the same kind as cans found in the Blackburns' farmhouse, as well as several sections out of a Toronto newspaper dated December 27, 1991. The same old newspaper had been found in the farmhouse missing the same sections. The pages of newspaper found in the bag were wrapped around human excrement similar to what was found in some of the break and enters. There were also numerous pages of meticulously neat military equipment lists similar to those seized in the other incidents. There was now a strong link between the farmhouse homicides, the break and enters and the kidnapping that all occurred in the area.

Ident had been able to lift fingerprints from some of the cottage break and enters, however, there was no match to any known criminal when police searched AFIS, Canada's Automated Fingerprint Identification System operated by the RCMP. We still didn't know who he was but we did know that the "House Hermit" was a strong suspect in the murders. The abduction victims' descriptions of the personality traits exhibited by their kidnapper were also consistent with those provided in the unknown-offender profile in the Blackburn case. I was confident of two things: this was our guy and he was going to kill again if we didn't catch him.

TO CATCH A KILLER

*"There is . . . nothing accomplished by any detective, that is
not the result of conscientious work, the exercise of human intelligence,
an efficient system of organization and intercommunication,
and good luck."*
—John Wilson Murray, *Memoirs of a Great Detective:
Incidents in the Life of John Wilson Murray*

I'm crouched low to the ground, hiding. My back is tight against a tree. My pulse is pounding in my ears. My heart feels like it's exploding out of my chest. My teeth are chattering. I can't stop shaking. Why am I so cold? I'm sweating so much. I want to lean out and look back. I can't hear him. I know he's close. He is going to kill me. I'm going to be the victim this time. This is the fear they feel. I'm going to be sick. A twig snaps behind me. I bolt. It's the last thing I remember.

AFTER I FINISHED VOMITING, I washed my face, brushed my teeth and shut off the bathroom light. Trapper, our yellow

Labrador retriever, was lying at the bottom of the bed when I came back into the bedroom.

As I got back into bed Bob rolled over and asked, "What was that all about?"

Trapper lifted his head as if waiting for an answer too. I'd obviously awakened the both of them.

"Just a bad dream."

"Stop reading cases before you go to bed."

I'd always had a poor memory and never liked to prepare for case consultations until the day before. I wanted the crime details fresh in my mind, but my workdays were now so busy that I had to bring the case materials home with me to be ready for the next day. Looking at reports and photographs had become my bedtime reading, but I took Bob's advice and stopped. I stayed at the office after regular work hours until I felt prepared for the next day. That put an end to the nightmares.

One thing that I always tried to do when brought into difficult cases like the Blackburn murders was to listen to what the cops thought was impeding their progress and success. By the time I was brought in most of the traditional avenues of investigation were usually already exhausted. Being able to contribute a new behavioural perspective in brainstorming sessions was one of my favourite exercises to participate in. I would endorse strategies that were often higher risk but that could pay huge dividends if successful. Being in the opinion business, taking risks was part of my job and I didn't shy away from being proactive, even if only to give luck the best possible chance to occur.

I encouraged the team to do a detailed media release including a photograph of the unique cryptic writings of this seeming
military buff, along with his physical description. Up until this
time, they'd held off releasing any evidentiary information. No
investigator likes to make their highly confidential evidence
public knowledge, but it was decided that the writings were so
distinctive that someone might remember them and feel compelled to call police. I thought it was well worth the evidence
hand-tipping risk. Their news release was delivered as front-
page headline news in the Toronto area the following day.
Despite the wide coverage, there was only one telephone call
received on the tip line. But in the end that one tip was all we
needed—it broke the case wide open.

Alison Shaw, originally from the town of Orangeville, contacted police after she read the media release in her Saturday
morning newspaper. It included a photograph of the Blackburns
and an illustration of the military notations. Having seen such
writings before, she felt absolutely certain that the man police
were looking for was David Snow. He was a friend of the family
and a former business partner of her husband. He was thirty-
seven years old and lived in Orangeville, only about twenty
kilometres away from Caledon. Snow had even at times babysat
their children. He was an antiques dealer and had an interest in
old timber frame homes. Alison described him as strange, eccentric and a loner. He didn't have a car so her husband gave him
rides. Neither Alison nor her husband had had contact with
Snow in some time.

About seven months earlier Alison and her husband had

been going through a storage hut in Orangeville once rented by Snow. It had been abandoned by him months earlier and no storage fees had been paid since. They bought the contents in the hope of recouping some losses from the husband's failed business partnership with him. They stumbled across a number of hard-core pornography magazines and videos, with themes of bondage, violence and pain and women as the victims. They also discovered a black notebook filled with distinctive military-type writings: lists of battleships, planes and a series of numbers beside them. They threw it all in the garbage.

It was extremely lucky that Alison had seen the newspaper that morning because she and her family were in the process of packing up and moving to Vancouver. She was leaving on the following Monday. If police had waited a couple more days to put out the release, Alison wouldn't have seen it.

Positive identification was made when police discovered a minor criminal history for Snow. It was an Orangeville charge of fraud by false pretenses related to writing bad cheques. His photograph and fingerprints had been taken but not yet submitted to the national database because he had not been convicted. He'd failed to appear on his court date. This information was also consistent with the comment made to the couple Snow had kidnapped before the Blackburns were murdered. The original prints were then compared to those unknown prints found in the cottage of the abduction victims. They were a match.

The police executed a search warrant at Snow's abandoned Orangeville home. They found sexually sadistic pornography everywhere and more military writings. The most important discovery was a briefcase containing photographs of the eight-sided barn on the Blackburns' farm. There was now a confirmed connection between Snow and the Blackburns.

Alison's husband advised police that a few years earlier he and his then business partner observed the octagonal barn on the Blackburns' farm one day when they were driving on the side roads of Caledon. They went in the driveway to the farm-house and met Ian and Nancy Blackburn, who had been sitting outside on the porch. The two men expressed their interest in dismantling the barn and reconstructing it elsewhere if they could find a buyer for it. They were allowed to have a closer look and even took photographs. The men left with an informal agreement that, if they found a buyer, they should come back and talk to Ian.

The OPP obtained a Canadawide warrant for Snow's arrest for the murders of Ian and Nancy Blackburn and a massive national manhunt for the armed and dangerous fugitive was launched. It wouldn't be very long before crimes similar to Snow's would resurface, albeit far beyond the jurisdiction of the OPP.

Over the summer, in the city of Vancouver, a young store clerk was brutally sexually assaulted but managed to escape, and then two young women—also working alone in small stores—were kidnapped. The abducted women were later found in a wooded area by RCMP officers, but the perpetrator had fled on foot. The women had been tied up, gagged and viciously sexually assaulted multiple times. One victim stated that she was forced to drive her attacker in her own car to the location in the woods where the first victim had already been held for eight days.

Police later found and searched her car. In it was a discarded train receipt for travel from Toronto to Vancouver on April 9, 1992, which was the day after the Blackburns went missing. It had been purchased in cash at the main train terminal, Union Station. Back in Toronto, Snow's photograph was shown to a ticket agent at the station and she remembered him because he had been arrogant and rude to her. In checking through the records it was found that Snow bought the one-way ticket to Vancouver. Our same sense of urgency in finding Snow was now being experienced by Vancouver police.

A few days later in Vancouver, at about 3:00 a.m., a fifty-three-year-old restaurant manager was confronted at gunpoint by Snow, who emerged from nearby woods as she was closing up. Snow forced her back inside the restaurant, but the building security alarm was not disarmed, prompting the security company to telephone. Snow let her answer the call; when she hung up he demanded money and stole cash from her wallet. Snow asked her if she had a car, and although hers was in the restaurant parking lot, she told him she didn't have one. He took her back outside behind the restaurant and struck her in the face and head when she attempted to fight him off. He bound her hands and ankles behind her back with nylons and gagged her. He then twisted wire around her neck and placed a plastic bag over her head. Just then police arrived—the employee's unusual responses to the security company's questions had caused them to raise the alarm. Snow fled but was captured a short time later.

Snow's victim was unconscious when she was discovered but she survived.

Of the twenty-five profile characteristics Ron and I had given to police, twenty-three of those matched Snow. Found guilty of multiple offences in British Columbia, he was declared a dangerous offender with an indefinite sentence given his determined public safety risk. Eventually he was returned to Ontario and entered pleas of guilty to break and enter, kidnapping, theft of money while in possession of a firearm and use of a firearm in the commission of an indictable offence. However, he pleaded not guilty to killing Ian and Nancy Blackburn. Six and a half years after their murders, a jury in Toronto found Snow guilty of two counts of first-degree murder. Snow was sentenced to life imprisonment with no chance of parole for twenty-five years.

David Snow remains a person of interest in several southern Ontario cold-case homicides that occurred during the same time frame as Ian and Nancy Blackburn were murdered and with many similar circumstances.

EVERYONE'S DAUGHTER

"Just a child
A victim of society gone wild
In God's grace
Please let me take her place . . ."
—From the song "Angel's Smile" by Brad French,
"for my little sister Kristen"

DURING THE TIME THAT I WAS WORKING on the Blackburn case, I was also squeezing in any spare moments that I had to get ready for my wedding. I was pleased that Bob's then twenty-year-old daughter also wanted to be a part of our ceremony. Cheryl was a beautiful young woman who credited me with healing the rift between her and her father after a period of tumultuous years following her parents' breakup. Not the usual role for the new woman in a divorced father's life, but I was glad to have played a part in bringing them back together.

Several weeks before the wedding, I got a call from Inspector Vince Bevan of the Niagara Regional Police. When he introduced himself on the phone I knew immediately who he was and hoped that he was looking for my help. I'd seen him in numerous media interviews over the last several months as he led a large multi-agency investigation in southern Ontario known as the Green Ribbon Task Force. Vince and I arranged to meet the next day so I could get a full briefing.

On Thursday, April 16, 1992, just before the Easter holiday long weekend, Kristen French left Holy Cross Catholic Secondary School in St. Catharines, Ontario, at about 2:45 p.m. in the drizzling rain. Normally she would have participated in after-school athletic activities such as precision skating or rowing, but the fifteen-year-old had been sidelined with a back injury. Kristen liked to get home as soon as she could after school to let out her dog.

When Kristen's mother, Donna, arrived home from work, Kristen wasn't there. This was out of character and her mother was immediately concerned. Donna called the school and spoke to the principal who then contacted some of Kristen's teachers and friends. No one had seen her since the end of school. The principal called Donna back and told her to call the police. As the evening went on, Donna and Kristen's father, Doug, knew something was terribly wrong.

Over the Easter weekend, four to five hundred police, teachers, students and members of the public gathered at Holy Cross school where a police command post had been set up to coordinate searches. Searchers found one shoe and a lock of hair—possibly cut with a knife during a struggle—believed to be

Kristen's in a church parking lot along her route home. Anyone who was in the vicinity of Kristen's route home at the time she went missing was asked to call police. Several witnesses came forward with information and the police pieced together the likelihood that Kristen was abducted. A young girl matching Kristen's description was seen walking along her route. A short time later, someone who knew Kristen reported having seen her talking to two men in a car that was pulled over on the side of the road. A few minutes later, another witness saw a man struggling with something in the back seat of a similarly described car, and others saw a similar car racing away from the area.

Holy Cross students gathered in large groups almost every day after Kristen went missing. The school was the site where the media congregated, so the students were coached on how to deal with reporters when bombarded with questions each day. As a coping mechanism, teachers organized activities such as composing prayers and poems. A Grade 9 student, Stephanie, wrote a prayer entitled "Colour Me Green."[4] The prayer identified green as the colour of hope that Kristen was safe. It was also the colour of the school's Cape Breton tartan for the girls' uniform skirts, which Kristen had been wearing at the time she went missing. The students decided to make up green ribbons to wear, symbolizing the hope that Kristen would return unharmed. The ribbons were enclosed in small packets along with a copy of the "Colour Me Green" prayer and distributed across the region.*

---

* The symbol of the "Green Ribbon of Hope" was later gifted from Holy Cross school and the French family to Child Find Canada as their national symbol of hope for all missing children.

Vince's task force was also named in honour of the students' campaign of hope.

On April 30, the hope of the French family and their community changed to anguish and despair when Kristen's body was discovered in a rural area along a roadside north of Burlington, Ontario. She had been sexually assaulted and died of asphyxia. Vince said, "All of the investigators worked so hard those first two weeks to find Kristen and we weren't successful. I was really worried about guys on the team, both men and women. They really thought we had a shot at bringing her home. They worked twenty-four hours a day to try and do that. And then when we found Kristen's body, they were devastated."

Less than a year earlier, in nearby Burlington, Leslie Mahaffy, fourteen, had attended an evening funeral home visitation for a friend who had died in a car accident and after the service she began walking toward home. Two weeks later her dismembered body was found in a lake near St. Catharines. Vince had been leading the Niagara piece of the investigation of Leslie's case and he recognized the similarities in the two cases.

Over the next several months the Green Ribbon Task Force combed through all of the leads from the public, probation and parole offices and other police agencies. But there was nothing of substance to give focus to possible suspects or information gleaned that forensically connected the two cases. When Vince and I met and he presented all of the information on both investigations, I agreed with his opinion that the two cases were likely connected. Forensic science was not linking them but the likenesses in criminal behaviour, including victim selection, crime motivation and execution, and basic geography were striking. Vince was getting ready to go to the public to solicit information, primarily regarding Kristen's murder, since there was significantly more information available in her case than Leslie's. He was developing a television show with a local independent television station, CHCH-TV, and asked for my help.

I was assigned a contact in the Green Ribbon Task Force: my old pal from our OPP recruit class, Sue Lloyd. We would be working with the show's producer, Rose Stricker. With a timeline of only several weeks to prepare, Rose, Sue and I, along with others, strategized to produce a show that would be persuasive for viewers to call in with tips. Our audience would be given factual information about what was and wasn't known about the case and dispel some widespread rumours. There would also be mention of a $100,000 reward for information. Our strategy was to evoke an emotional response in the viewers through re-enactments, poignant interviews of friends and family reliving memories of Kristen, as well as scripted voiceovers to go along with the case-file video footage. We wanted to be factual, but nonsensational. Dan McLean, a trusted local news anchor, was selected as the show's host.

By the time I'd been brought in on the investigation, an FBI unknown-offender profile had already been prepared by Gregg McCrary of the BSU in Quantico, and he agreed to be part of the television program.[5] In consultation with the FBI, it was decided to release previously confidential information contained in their profile. We decided to release only the details that we were confident had the highest change of being accurate.

Details of Kristen's life were shared with the audience in emotional interviews. Donna was interviewed at home in Kristen's bedroom with it looking just the way that she had last left it. Her bed was perfectly made with teddy bears sitting on top. Donna said, "I just don't have the heart to put anything away yet. Right now, it would be like packing away my memories and I just can't do that. I like her room just as it is now. I often come in and I'll sit and talk to her or just think about her. What really gets tough is when you think of the things that will never come. The fact that she will never marry and won't be able to plan a wedding. She was in a wedding a couple of years ago and when they went trying on bridesmaids' dresses, she found a wedding dress that she just loved and I said, 'Try it on Kristen.' She tried it on and she looked so beautiful. In October Kristen was to be a bridesmaid again and they went and chose their dresses and ordered them. They were green. That's the hardest part—just thinking ahead. Things that you won't be able to do. Had she been older, and [had] she had a child, at least I'd [have] had a granddaughter by her."

I was videotaped at the sites of Kristen's abduction and the place where her body was found. I made several pleas for an elderly couple to come forward with their information, as several other witnesses had seen them close to the abduction scene. Gregg McCrary was brought into the show from a Washington, DC, studio via live video feed, with a photograph of the United States

Capitol building in the background. I knew Gregg from my time at the FBI and we shared the strong belief that the offenders responsible for these deaths would watch the show. It was an opportunity for us to drive a wedge between the two of them. Gregg was focused on messaging to the public and to the offenders that we knew their profiles, were confident that the case would be solved and the offenders caught.

Gregg advised viewers that this was a high-risk, sexually motivated homicide. The offenders stalked Kristen in advance and would have done the same with other young girls in the past. It appeared that Kristen may have been conned toward the car perhaps by one of them asking for directions. Other young women may have experienced similar interactions and he encouraged them to call police if they had.

Gregg reiterated that eyewitnesses had seen two males inside the abduction vehicle. As I had cautioned investigators in the Blackburn case, Gregg told viewers that an opinion in relation to age was difficult and determined more behaviourally than chronologically. They would likely be in their late twenties or early thirties.

One of the offenders would be the leader and the other more of a follower. The dominant offender was a human predator and would be a psychopath. He would be the one behind the crime and the "cold-blooded killer." He would feel no guilt or remorse for the suffering of the victims or their families.

If this dominant offender had a wife or girlfriend, he would be the dominant one in the relationship. It would be an abusive relationship as he demonstrated he had a hatred for women. He would have a history of criminal sexual deviancy, including sexual assaults, and would likely have spent time in prison for sex-related crimes.

Given the evidence, this dominant offender would likely be employed in a semi-skilled industrial setting, working with power tools, and probably with a workshop at home.

Gregg provided the opinion that the secondary offender would have a very close but subservient relationship with the main offender. That person's crime motivation may have been more the thrill of committing the crimes. He was more likely to feel emotional over the killings, fear, apprehension and have a problem coping with the aftermath of the crimes. Gregg warned that the secondary person should be fearful for his own safety from the dominant offender.

Near the end of the segment, Dan asked Gregg about the dominant offender. "If he is watching tonight, what do you think he might be experiencing?" Gregg replied, "The only thing the dominant offender cares about is apprehension. If he is watching, I want to tell him that you are going to be apprehended. It's just a question of when."

Filming of the ninety-minute show wrapped up the day before my wedding and I hurried home in time to get to the rehearsal dinner. Thankfully Bob and our families and friends had pitched in to look after most of the last-minute details. The next day as my mother helped me get dressed in my wedding gown, I remembered what Donna had said about Kristen trying on the wedding dress. I was experiencing one of the happiest days of my life, a day with my mother that Donna would never experience with Kristen.

The Abduction of Kristen French aired on July 21, 1992, a little more than three months after Kristen disappeared. The satellite company broadcast the program unscrambled across North America. Bob and I were away on our honeymoon, but I called back to the task force office the next morning to scc if the elderly couple who had witnessed Kristen's abduction, and that I had made the appeal to, had called in. They hadn't, but thirty thousand others had.

Not having anticipated such a response, there was no planned capacity to deal with that number of tips and the task force was swamped. Receiving so many tips was a double-edged sword. The more tips received, the better the chance that one or more would advance the investigation—but there were so many it was hard to know where to start. RCMP officer and intelligence analyst Larry Wilson was one of the forty-one call takers the night of the show and later daily assigned leads to dozens of investigators to follow up on. The thirty thousand tips grew to over forty-one thousand in the weeks and months that followed and three thousand persons of interest were identified. Out of necessity, Larry developed a suspect management system to prioritize the persons of interest. He later developed the Persons of Interest Priority Assessment Tool (POIPAT)[6]—a manual that assists police to create their own objective and consistent priority ranking of suspects according to the unique nature of their particular investigation.

———

In the end it wouldn't be a tip that broke the case. In January 1993, twenty-two-year-old Karla Homolka, whose co-workers and family disbelieved her story that her black-and-blue face had been the result of a car accident, was forced to contact police and report she had been the victim of a domestic assault. Her twenty-eight-year-old husband, Paul Bernardo, was arrested. This disclosure began a snowballing series of events that led to the arrest of both of them for the murders of Leslie Mahaffy and Kristen French and numerous sexual assaults of others. No one could have imagined, not even we so-called expert profilers, that it would be this woman and her husband.

Homolka's defence counsel entered into a plea bargain with the Crown attorney's office that would come to be known as the "Deal with the Devil." In consideration of the need to have her testify against her husband, and prior to having full knowledge of her involvement in the crimes, a deal was made that Homolka would plead guilty to her involvement in the crimes and serve only twelve years in prison.

The police, Crown attorneys and public would be continually shocked as each new piece of information of her husband's criminal activity came to light, much of it videotaped, including:

- Bernardo was responsible for a series of brutal sexual assaults in the Toronto area that began in 1987, but he slipped through the cracks of a task force investigation;
- complicit with Homolka, Bernardo had sexually assaulted her fifteen-year-old sister, Tammy, who had been so heavily

drugged that she died (at the time the death was ruled accidental);

- Bernardo stalked several women in St. Catharines and committed further sexual assaults there;
- Bernardo stalked, sexually assaulted and murdered Leslie Mahaffy; and
- complicit with Homolka, Bernardo stalked, sexually assaulted and murdered Kristen French

Ron MacKay and Toronto forensic psychiatrist Peter Collins worked extensively with the task force in setting up an interview strategy for the psychopathic sexual sadist and assisted in the preparation of the search warrant for his residence. Timing of the two events was critical. I was out of the country on vacation and had hoped to be back in time to help out, but the proverbial shit hit the fan when Bernardo's name and his impending arrest were leaked to the press. All plans were accelerated and officers were not as prepared as they could have been to interview him or execute the search warrant on his home. This situation compromised almost all of the behaviourally based strategies that the guys had been working on.

Bernardo's interview was not a success, as far as getting him to confess to the crimes, but a great deal of evidence was found in his house. After the police completed seventy-one days of searching and the warrant expired, Bernardo instructed his lawyer to search a location in the house that somehow had been missed. Videotapes were recovered that were eventually turned over to Vince and he was told, "I feel sorry for anyone who has to watch that." The lawyer never would have spoken a truer word. The tapes contained recordings of the multiple victims of sexual sadistic assaults and torture. They also revealed the depth of Homolka's previously undisclosed involvement in the crimes, but unfortunately the "Deal with the Devil" had already been made.

The FBI profile was fairly accurate, with inaccuracies accounted for by misinterpreting evidence or well-intentioned, but incorrect, eyewitness accounts. Homolka advised police that she and Bernardo had watched the television show and had even recorded it. Coincidentally, Gregg realized that he, along with John Douglas and Ron MacKay, who was at the time an FBI police fellow-in-training, had profiled seven of the Toronto-area sexual assaults dating back to 1987 and 1988.[7]

Prior to the start of Bernardo's jury trial, Vince asked Ron MacKay, Peter Collins and me to consult with him and the Crown prosecutors regarding their trial strategy and how to introduce the videotaped evidence of Bernardo's assaults on his victims. We provided the prosecution team with our opinions on presenting the evidence in court and how to cross-examine Bernardo when he testified on his own behalf. We knew a psychopath like him would insist on taking advantage of a grandstanding opportunity. We were in the court to watch the jury members' faces during Bernardo's pitiful attempts to explain and even justify his actions. After everything they had seen and heard during the trial, the twelve men and women on the jury were not about to be duped—they found him guilty of all the charges brought against him and he was jailed indefinitely as a dangerous offender.

———

After Bernardo's trial was over there was a public outcry. People wanted to know how this serial predator and his accomplice spouse, who committed such a multitude of crimes throughout southern Ontario, could evade justice for over five years. In 1995 the Honourable Mr. Justice Archie Campbell of the Superior Court of Justice in Ontario led an inquiry into the serial sexual assault investigations in and around Toronto, the homicides in the St. Catharines area, as well as issues that were raised regarding Ontario's forensic testing capacities and forensic pathology examinations. The government requested that he identify issues and make recommendations that would improve such investigations in the future.

I asked to appear before Justice Campbell to share information about an innovative investigative tool that I was already aware of that could increase the capacity of police to investigate these types of crimes. Since 1993 the computerized Violent Crime Linkage Analysis System (ViCLAS) had been operating across Canada. Ron MacKay spearheaded the research and development of the program, similar to the FBI's ViCAP program in the US, and consulted me in the process. Specialized analytical units were set up across the country. Police officers with specialized training analyzed submitted violent crime cases, such as homicides, sexual assaults and other violent crimes from across the country. Those cases with similar offender behaviour, description, victimology, geographic location and offence dynamics were flagged. The analysts then notified the submitting agencies of the potential links in their cases in an effort to track and identify serial offenders at the earliest possible opportunity. The ability existed to identify involved agencies so that they could pool their investigative and financial resources to work together on finding offenders. The OPP formed a small five-person ViCLAS who I helped train, and I consulted with them regularly.

Despite the ability to identify serial sex offenders and killers at the earliest opportunity, there was one huge problem that ViCLAS couldn't wrestle to the ground: nobody was using it, including my own agency. Ron and I had made presentations on behalf of the program to chiefs of police across Ontario and they all agreed to support the program, however, ViCLAS was failing dismally with few criteria cases actually being submitted by their investigators. I suggested to Justice Campbell that he recommend the Ontario government make it mandatory that police agencies promptly submit crimes that fit the ViCLAS criteria. He agreed that if agencies involved in the investigation of Bernardo had had the system in place, and then used it throughout the investigation, linkages between many of these crimes would have been identified. Then agencies could have shared their resources and worked together to solve the crimes. Perhaps assault victims could have been spared their ordeal and even lives saved. We were too late for Tammy Homolka, Leslie Mahaffy and Kristen French.

Several years later I was in Kingston for some meetings and was invited to take a tour of Kingston Penitentiary, often referred to as Canada's Alcatraz. It was always an uncomfortable feeling for me to hand over my gun before entering a prison facility, especially when you knew that some of your former "clients" were inside and could be roaming about. I didn't see any of mine until my last stop, the segregation unit. There was no roaming around in there. Everyone was on twenty-three-hour-a-day lockdown in their one-and-a-half-by-three-metre cells. The cell bars were also covered with Plexiglas, apparently for the protection of loathed inmates, on the lowest rung of inmate hierarchy. I had just stepped inside the unit's observation dome and was chatting with one of the guards when I glanced across the hall and saw Bernardo sitting on his bunk. I watched him for about five minutes, but he never looked over. He was watching a small portable television, constantly changing channels every few seconds with his TV remote. It felt good to see that a television was the only thing left in his life that he could control.

BEHAVIOURAL SCIENCES SECTION

*"In most cases being a good boss means hiring talented people
and then getting out of their way."*
—Tina Fey, *Bossypants*

IN 1994 I MOVED FROM TORONTO to Orillia, about 130
kilometres to the north, where the OPP was building its new
headquarters. Bob had transferred over from Toronto police to
make the move with me and before long he was working in a
new provincial anti-biker squad. We bought a large home just
outside Orillia and, at Bob's suggestion, my parents moved
into the lower level. Not long after, Dad became ill with several
different health issues, accompanied by an aggressive onset of
dementia, and he died in January 1995. It was a sad time for
our family, but I was glad to have been able to spend a lot of
time together in the last months of his life.

I was working out of a retrofitted industrial warehouse in the
west end of Orillia until my new office in headquarters was ready

for me to move in. Again I was tucked back in the corner of a maze of CIB offices with my FBI graduation certificate hanging behind my desk and Mr. De Niro's smiling face not too far away. But my "me" wall was filling up with other training certificates, plus I was collecting my own "attagirl" accolade plaques recognizing my assistance to their investigations. My allotment of one filing cabinet had long been filled and now even my office floor space was at a premium with overflowing boxes of case files, autopsy reports, photographs and anything else investigators wanted me to take a look at.

I'd barely settled into my chair one Monday morning when my phone rang. OPP Chief Superintendent Gerry Boose asked me to come to his office right away then hung up. The chief's office was just down the hall from CIB so I didn't have much time to consider what trouble I might be in.

Our meeting lasted all of two minutes. He said that the OPP was restructuring and they wanted to be ready for the anticipated recommendations coming out in the release of Justice Campbell's "Bernardo Investigation Review." Because of the success I'd had in profiling he wanted to form a new OPP section that would specialize in providing behavioural-oriented support services to criminal investigators across Ontario. He asked me what I thought. "Yes, sir," I replied. "I think that is an excellent idea." (Momma didn't raise no fool, as the saying goes.) He asked me to put together a proposal for the new section and have it back to him as soon as possible. I had only one question. "Can I be the boss?" He replied, "You'd seem to be the logical choice, so yes."

Being at the helm of the first Behavioural Sciences Section (BSS) in Canada when it opened for business in June 1995 was one of the highlights of my career. I wanted to stay actively involved in casework as well as run the section but needed help, so I hired Jim Van Allen as the OPP's second criminal profiler. I'd done my homework on Jim, who had spent most of his career in northern Ontario. He possessed a strong criminal investigation background, had the reputation of being a risk taker with confidence, and his training and skills were very different from mine—a big reason why I wanted him on my team. Since the FBI no longer hosted the fellowship training program, I enrolled Jim in a new two-year understudy and accreditation program sponsored by the International Criminal Investigative Analysis Fellowship (ICIAF), our profilers' association. (Current ICIAF and FBI profilers, along with those retired and working for former BSU chief Roger Depue's company, the Academy Group, provided classroom training and field study placements.)

I knew right away that one unit BSS could use was Polygraph because their talents went far beyond their technical expertise. Aside from being able to spot lies based on physiological responses to questions when suspects were hooked up to a polygraph, these guys knew how to talk to people, and were masters at breaking down defence mechanisms with their persuasive techniques. They'd been honing their own form of behavioural analysis skills when I was still running up and down the highway arresting drunks in Port Credit.

The fledgling ViCLAS Unit, still struggling to get off the ground, was another no-brainer for the team. I knew what they were capable of and was confident their caseload would soon be going through the roof. Sure enough, when Justice Campbell released his report a year later, not only were violent crime submissions made mandatory in Ontario's Police Services Act, I also had a budget increase of over $4 million to set up an Ontario ViCLAS Centre. My staff of five grew to forty uniformed and civilian personnel.

Dr. Peter Collins joining us was another police first in Canada. His Forensic Psychiatry Unit added a much-needed psychiatric and mental health perspective to our investigation support services. Medical science was a perfect alliance with all that we were offering behaviourally. Peter had not only worked with Ron MacKay and me on the murder of Kristen French, he had also assisted Ron in the development of ViCLAS. He had a solid resume with particular expertise in sexual deviance and violent crime from having already worked for years with the RCMP and police in Ottawa, Toronto and the Niagara Region.

Stalking behaviour is the hallmark of so many serial predators, with Bernardo being a notable example. Criminal harassment legislation had been in place since 1993, but it still needed to be taken more seriously by the police, judiciary and the public. Factors present in cases needed to be better understood as warning signs and indicators of potential future violence. Again a first in the country, the Threat Assessment Unit worked with victims, police and other agencies where future risk of harm could be prevented, mitigated or, if already existing, better managed. Ontario's Correctional Services assigned one of their probation and parole officers to work directly with us. It was a particularly proud day when I got a call asking for the new unit to work with the Ontario Parole Board and provide training to help them better understand offenders' past criminal behaviours and potential future dangerousness should they be released back into the community.

Geographic profiling had first come on my radar when Ron MacKay introduced me to Vancouver PD officer Kim Rossmo. Based on environmental criminology, mathematics and his investigative experience, Kim had developed a computerized geographic profiling system that predicted where a serial offender lived in relation to their crime scenes. In simple terms, once a series of crimes were determined to be committed by the same person, the location of each crime was input into the system, spatially analyzed, and a map produced highlighting the general

Me, Roy Hazelwood, Ron MacKay, 1997

location of where the offender was likely to reside. Like criminal profiling and ViCLAS, it helped identify and prioritize persons of interest living in the area identified for investigators to follow up on. Kim agreed to train one of my officers and geographic profiling was added to our repertoire.

Sometimes I found team members in unexpected places. I'd gone back to my alma mater, University of Toronto, and took courses to complete their Crime and Deviance major. One of my psychology professors asked me to come back and speak to one of his other classes about my work as a criminal profiler and the new BSS. After that class I was approached by one of his students, Angela Eke, and we talked at length about her under-graduate research in offender profiling. We kept in touch over the years as she pursued her master's thesis on the impact of stalking on victims and her PhD thesis on staging in homicide cases. I was always impressed with the rigor of her research and how it fit in with what BSS was doing, so I was happy to have Angela accept my invitation to work for me part-time while she completed her studies. I'd seen first-hand the advantages of the FBI's research partnerships with academia and mental health professionals and wanted to establish that legitimacy here in Canada. A formal research unit was eventually estab-lished with Dr. Angela Eke heading it up.

After BSS had been up and running for a few years I received a card in the mail from a superior court judge before whom I'd appeared in a homicide trial. He said he had just read an article on the work being conducted in the BSS and complimented me and my staff. "I hope that your success and coordinated consolidation of services has continued," he said. "As a trial judge, I am most appreciative of helpful, reliable input to a standard of excellence."[8] To know that our work was having an effect on the whole justice system was the ultimate compliment.

I'd been president of the ICIAF since 1997 and each year BSS hosted an international conference on violent crime cosponsored by the OPP, RCMP and ICIAF. Similar to the Quantico National Academy consultations, local police were encouraged not only to register for the conference but also to bring along their unsolved violent crime cases to be reviewed by attending ICIAF profilers. Lawyers, psychologists, psychiatrists and forensic experts who were either attending or speaking at the conference were often asked to sit in on the evening consultations. Rather than host the event in a large city, we instead spent the week at a tranquil rustic lodge on Lake Simcoe, south of Orillia. Any spare time after our classes or consultations was spent letting off steam playing basketball or baseball—pretty much always Canada against the US, with a few stray country ringers.

The conference always opened with a perspective of crime that many often didn't get to hear—that of the victims and their families. When an investigation was completed most officers and civilians went back to dealing with the multitude of other cases they'd been assigned. They rarely interacted with victims or their families and I wanted to make sure those perspectives were not ignored. So the first session of each conference was a "survivor" story. The presentations demonstrated how victims and families moved on from their tragic circumstances to have positive achievements in their personal and professional lives. Many had gone on to become advocates and effect change in Canada's criminal justice system.

Doug and Donna French spoke at the first conference we hosted. There was the tragic story of their daughter's murder to tell, but they also wanted Kristen's life to be known and remembered—her enjoyment of team sports like precision skating and rowing; her beloved dog, Sasha; her excitement about having her first boyfriend over to cook him dinner and wanting Dad, Mom and her brother out of the house before he arrived. They were all stories that Doug and Donna chose to remember Kristen by rather than dwelling on the evil done to take her away from them. They told the good stories that

Doug French, Lesley Rice, Donna French, me

followed the tragedy, about the many wonderful people they met and their acts of kindness, great and small.

There was the young Holy Cross student who knocked on their front door when Kristen was still missing and asked if he could cut their lawn for them. Donna thanked him but told him that their lawn mower wasn't working. He left but came back a short time later in a pickup truck with his father. They'd brought their own lawn mower over and the father and son cut the grass. Donna had them stay to have dinner with her and Doug before they returned home.

On another day, Donna was home alone when an elderly man knocked on the front door. It was shortly after Kristen had been found and the man wanted only to say how sorry he was and to shake Donna's hand.

Several years after Kristen's murder, a stranger came up to Doug when he was sitting in a Tim Hortons coffee shop with some friends having a coffee. The man asked him if he was Kristen French's father and he said that he was. The man expressed his condolences and then gave him an envelope. Inside was a ten-dollar Tim Hortons gift card to buy Doug and his friends coffee next time.

In 2001 I was in Calgary visiting some family members and was introduced to the hockey player Sheldon Kennedy. My brief conversation with Sheldon ended with me inviting him to come to Ontario to open our upcoming conference. Sheldon wasn't going to be telling a story similar to past guest speakers. At the time he was barely surviving—and that's why I wanted him to come.

Sheldon was a Manitoba native who'd played in various hockey leagues for almost fifteen years. He'd been a member of three NHL teams over eight years and in 1996 was playing for the Calgary Flames when he made the gut-wrenching decision to come forward with allegations of sexual abuse by his junior league coach. For years Sheldon had felt that if he disclosed the abuse he would not be believed. However, he finally felt comfortable and confident enough to speak with an officer he met with Calgary Police Service. Another player came forward as well, but his name was never made public. The charges filed against the coach were a severe blow to the reputation of Canada's beloved national sport.

At one time Sheldon was seen as a rising star in the NHL but off the ice he had been spiralling downward. From the age of sixteen he had been arrested every few years for some criminal behaviour related to alcohol or drug use, including marijuana, cocaine and crystal meth. Having sustained numerous physical injuries, his contract with the Calgary Flames was not renewed. He tried to make a hockey comeback but bounced between teams and leagues for a couple of more years before he finally hung up his skates in 1999.

I met Sheldon for breakfast on the morning of the first day of the conference and he was clearly still struggling with his addiction demons. His eyes were bloodshot, his face flushed, and he looked like he hadn't slept at all the night before. A couple of cigarettes and coffees did little to settle his nerves. He was concerned that he hadn't done a lot of public speaking and wouldn't do a good job for me. Given his past brushes with the law, I supposed that appearing before a bunch of cops was only adding to his angst.

I told him, "Just tell your story and you'll be fantastic." And he was.

For the first hour, Sheldon paced back and forth at the front of the conference room, microphone in hand and head down. He rarely looked up from the floor. He started by telling of growing up in rural Manitoba and learning to play hockey on a frozen backyard pond. Despite his lack of polished presentation skills, he endeared himself to his audience within minutes.

Sheldon spoke of his passion for hockey and that he knew he was good at it. Each summer he looked forward to getting away from the family farm and attending hockey school. When he was fourteen, Sheldon met a coach, Graham James, at one of the schools. James was an ex-schoolteacher who was then a scout and considered influential in junior hockey league circles in the Prairies and across Canada. The coach changed Sheldon's life in ways he could never have imagined.

Sheldon's presentation was raw and filled with emotion. Halfway through the morning we took a break. He was the only speaker I ever recall receiving a spontaneous standing ovation at coffee break.

When we returned to the conference room, Sheldon continued with a story that was all too familiar to those of us who worked on these types of cases. If I checked off the list of characteristics and behaviours that FBI agent Ken Lanning taught me to look for years earlier during my training in Quantico, James had every one of them. The charismatic coach engaged in all the classic sexual-grooming behaviours of a predator. He "courted" Sheldon's parents by praising their son's hockey capabilities. His parents believed James could positively influence Sheldon's future in the sport and were excited that he would take such an interest in their child. Sheldon confided in James that his father ruled his home with tough love tactics that matched his temper. Sheldon therefore relished the kind of caring attention James gave him. After hockey camp was over, James invited Sheldon to participate in a tournament in Winnipeg. Sheldon's parents were thrilled that the coach had even invited their son to stay at his apartment. Sheldon's world came crashing down the first night he stayed there.

In the months that followed, James's seduction progressed from his initial sexual touching to multiple sexual assaults on Sheldon. All the while, James instilled in Sheldon that he was the key to his hockey future, and without him he would achieve nothing. Given the reputation of James in the Canadian minor hockey world, Sheldon believed him. He was trapped in a nightmare of compromise that he couldn't wake up from.

Sheldon not only suffered from the sexual assaults but also from the resulting emotional upheaval that he had in common with so many victims who go through similar abuse. James isolated Sheldon from his family and friends. Sheldon hated himself, feeling guilty and ashamed for what he was prepared to endure to realize his dream of playing professional hockey. Over the next three years Sheldon turned to alcohol and drugs to help him cope and even contemplated suicide. At nineteen years of age Sheldon finally got away from James when he started to play for his first NHL team, the Detroit Red Wings.

There were many other sexual abuse allegations that could have been disclosed by other hockey players against James but those players chose not to come forward at that time. Sheldon wouldn't betray the trust of any of his teammates who confided in him by publicly speaking of what he knew. In 1997, just a few months after the allegations were made, James pleaded guilty and received a three-and-a-half-year sentence for his hundreds of assaults on Sheldon and the other unnamed player. James went from being *Hockey News* magazine's 1989 Man of the Year to the status of convicted child sex offender and banned from coaching hockey in Canada. He served only eighteen months of his sentence and completed his parole in 2000. (A few years later Canadians would again be outraged, not only with the news of more NHL players filing sexual assault charges against James, but also when they learned that after he had finished his sentence in relation to the hundreds of assaults on Sheldon and his teammate, James had quietly been given a pardon by the National Parole Board.)

At the end of his presentation that day to the packed conference room, Sheldon revealed what he regretted more than anything else his abuser had done to him. "He stole my love of hockey and I was never able to get that back," An even longer standing ovation followed and for the first time that morning Sheldon smiled.

I kept in touch with Sheldon over the years and watched him journey to a very different place in his life. He gained momentum in his outspoken efforts to raise awareness of child sexual abuse, such as appearing before government committees in Canada and the US examining such issues as sexual abuse in organized sports, minimum penalties for sex offenders and eliminating pardons for sex offenders. Sheldon once told me, "We also need to have things in place to turn these victims' lives around so that they don't end up in our system."

Sheldon went on to be voted Calgary's Citizen of the Year and had a child advocacy centre named after him. Best of all he achieved success at keeping his substance abuse demons at bay. The last time I spoke to him he said, "I can tell a solution story now and not just the Sheldon story." Whether speaking before cops in a conference room or in a parliamentary committee hearing room, Sheldon's story made a difference. I still occasionally see him on television speaking out on the issues that are important to him. He seems a polished professional with lots of confidence and doesn't speak with his head down anymore. It's held high, as it should be.

CHRISTOPHER AND THE LAW

*"I alone cannot change the world, but I can cast a stone
across the waters to create many ripples."*
—Mother Teresa

JIM STEPHENSON ALWAYS TOOK THE LEAD in telling the
story. He's had years of experience doing public speaking engagements and media interviews. On most occasions when Jim was
speaking, his wife, Anna, was by his side. In years past, they
would often be wearing buttons on their lapels with a picture of
their eleven-year-old son, Christopher, in his hockey uniform
and the slogan "Never again. The laws must change."

Jim had spoken at an ICIAF conference as one of my "survivor" guest speakers and he and Anna and I had become friends.
One morning I stopped in to see them at their Brampton home.
As usual, the three of us sat around their kitchen table to visit.
Anna made coffee and set a plate of scones and pastries in the
middle of the table, pushing it just a little closer to my reach. We
chatted about our families and their upcoming trip to visit their

daughter, Amanda, who was born three years after Christopher. She was now married and living in Australia.

Our conversation drifted to the topic of Christopher and on this occasion Anna was the one to speak first about something that I had never privately heard them talk about before: the night of Friday, June 17, 1988. As she spoke, she occasionally shut her eyes, seeing it in her mind all over again.

"That night I went with Amanda and Christopher to the mall," Anna said. "Christopher needed a haircut and we were getting some stuff for Father's Day on the weekend. We did some shopping and then went to the hairdresser where we usually go. I asked the girl if she would have time to cut Christopher's hair. It was about a quarter to nine so she said there wasn't much time left before the mall would be closing at nine. She said if we came back tomorrow morning she would take him first thing. We agreed to do that.

"Right across the hall was a sewing centre. I needed some ribbon for Amanda's dress for my brother's wedding in a few weeks. She was in the wedding party. We had a lot of parcels from our shopping and it was a very tiny shop so I asked Christopher to wait at the door. Amanda came into the shop with me and the lady showed me where the ribbon was. I had my back to the door while I was looking. They didn't have what I wanted so Amanda and I came back out to the hallway. Christopher was gone."

The hairdresser next door was just closing up her shop and Anna asked if by chance Christopher was with her. She said he wasn't but just a couple of minutes earlier she had seen him walking away with an older man. She said the man had his arm around him and that Christopher looked upset. Anna asked the hairdresser to call security and left Amanda with her while she ran and searched the hallways nearby. Within a few minutes security arrived and they called Peel Regional Police.

Anna said, "I was in such a panic. I had a gut feeling that something was really wrong. I was shaking and I remember thinking about that little boy, Adam Walsh. I thought this couldn't be happening. I was kind of out of it as I know I kept repeating myself. The officer actually took my hand and asked me to tell him what clothes Christopher had on. When he touched my hand, even though it was just for a brief moment, it made me feel a bit better. I thought okay, everything is going to be okay and they will find Christopher."

After giving a description of Christopher to the police officers who were on scene at the mall, Anna and Amanda were taken to the police station. Jim was contacted by police and met them there.

Anna said, "I always remember that night—Amanda and Christopher were arguing and I told them they better behave while we were shopping. To this day, I feel guilty that I yelled at both of them that night because they were fighting. And I feel so guilty that I left Christopher at the door. I still feel so guilty." Anna stopped then and asked Jim for some tissues to wipe away her tears.

I wasn't surprised that Jim immediately wanted to follow up on Anna's comment. "I don't know how many times I had taken the kids to a mall or plaza," he said. "I'd take them to the toy section of the store and tell them to stay there and look at the toys. I'd go to menswear or the hardware section or whatever. I'd sometimes leave them for twenty minutes or a half hour. I'd come back and they'd be fine. Those were different days and different times.

"This was not the first time that Christopher had been missing in a shopping mall. When he was probably about four, maybe five, we had taken him to another mall. At some point in the evening I thought he was with Anna and she thought he was with me. It was near closing time when we realized he had wandered off. We walked around as the shoppers were going home and the crowd was getting smaller and smaller. Finally it was just Anna and I walking around looking for Christopher and we kept wondering where he could be. It never even occurred to us that someone would have taken him. Then we looked down the hallway and we saw this big security guard walking toward us with our little boy. We thanked the security guard and went home."

The next day police released a composite drawing of the man after interviewing the hairdresser and also a young hockey player from Christopher's minor league team who had seen them leaving the mall. Following the abduction's being the top story on Saturday's six o'clock news, two tips were received in the hunt for the white male, between fifty and sixty years of age, about five feet tall, thin, with grey hair and a bald spot. The physical description and police composite drawing were identified as looking like Joseph Fredericks, a forty-eight-year-old convicted pedophile and psychopath with a long history of violence and sexual offences against children. One of the tips was from a former roommate and the other came from his parole officer.

Fredericks had spent over twenty years in a psychiatric hospital and had recently been released from a federal prison. Days earlier he had moved a second time since his release, to Brampton, and, because of some bureaucratic mix-ups with Corrections Canada, the local police had not been aware he was residing in their area.

Those tips led to Fredericks' arrest at his home on Sunday morning and he was interviewed by Peel homicide officers Ron Bain and Len Favreau. A great amount of physical evidence of Christopher having been in the residence was found, and Fredericks confessed to killing the boy—and then took the detectives to Christopher's body in a nearby field.

With Ron and Len still with Fredericks, other officers came to Jim and Anna's home to tell them the worst-possible news: that Christopher had been murdered and that his body had been found. Jim and Anna would later learn that Christopher had been abducted at knifepoint by Fredericks. He was initially taken to a field near the mall and sexually assaulted. Fredericks then took Christopher to a room he had rented in the basement of a Brampton family's home. They went in through a separate back entrance and he kept the boy bound in a downstairs room for almost twenty-four hours. The family was home upstairs throughout and never heard a thing. Christopher was beaten and sexually assaulted multiple times. Fredericks then walked him approximately seven kilometres to another field, and again sexually assaulted and then killed him. Christopher died from a cut to his left carotid artery.

Jim said, "Being told on the Sunday afternoon of Father's

Day, sitting in my living room, that Christopher was dead was the lowest point of my life." Days later Jim found a hand-drawn picture in Christopher's room that was his Father's Day card.

Jim and Anna talked about how their religious faith and the strength of their relationship helped get them through the days that followed. Their lives with each other and eight-year-old Amanda were going to be forever changed by Christopher's absence but they had to somehow go on. After a couple of weeks, Jim went back to coaching Christopher's baseball team. At the end of the school year a few weeks later, he and Anna went to Christopher's school to pick up his report card.

Fredericks' murder trial took place in the fall of 1989. Because of all the case publicity, the trial venue was changed to Stratford, about 120 kilometres southwest of Brampton. During the trial Jim and Anna often met for dinner with the investigating officers, Ron and Len. One evening conversation stands out in their minds. It followed a particularly difficult day for them sitting in the court and listening to expert testimony from a psychiatrist. They were extremely frustrated with the testimony from the doctor who said everyone knew Fredericks was dangerous and yet he'd been let out of jail two-thirds of the way through his sentence. Jim said, "I still remember Len looked across the table at me and asked, 'Mr. Stephenson, would you like to see things change?' I expected that he would say that they and the Crown and the Attorney General would do what was necessary to make sure that this kind of release of dangerous people wouldn't happen again. But instead, Len looked back at me, and I will never forget it, he said, 'Well, if you want to see things change, Mr. Stephenson, you're going to have to do it yourself. You're going to have to be an advocate for change.'"

I'd had these same types of candid conversations with families in the past. A police officer, Crown attorney, advocacy group and all others with the best of intentions could lobby for change, but the face of a child and the first-hand story told by a family had by far the greatest impact and influence on government decision makers. To politicize the tragic loss of a loved one for the sake of a greater good was no easy decision for a family. It was exhausting, frustrating, expensive, and could take years to realize any success, if at all. And yet it was no surprise to me that Jim and Anna were up for it.

Fredericks was convicted of first-degree murder and sentenced to life in prison with no chance of parole for twenty-five years. He launched an appeal but it was never dealt with because Fredericks ended up being murdered by a fellow inmate.

An inquest into Christopher's death was later called. It lasted five months. When the recommendations came out, it was time for the Stephensons' personal advocacy efforts to officially begin.

Jim said, "I don't think we really understood advocacy until after the inquest. As valid and substantial as the inquest recommendations were, they weren't going to go anywhere unless somebody went forward with them. As I look back on it, we didn't form an organization to address what broke down in the system. I wanted us to be a family that was speaking to the government representatives rather than to have it be the president of some organization. That was effective for us in the long run.

"The coolness of the justice system, particularly the federal justice system, was difficult to understand. They just seemed to be kind of cavalier. They didn't even say they were sorry. I remember meeting with the minister of justice and I got really upset with him. He told us, 'Unfortunately your son just happened to be at the wrong place at the wrong time.' I said, 'No. You're wrong. Christopher was at the right place at the right time. Joseph Fredericks was at the wrong place at the wrong time. That was an oversight of the corrections system.'

"The conversation didn't go much further than that. But that was kind of typical of the way the federal government reacted to us. We didn't ask for an apology for all the things that went wrong but it would have been nice to have. The most we got was a letter from the prime minister saying he was sorry about our tragic loss."

One of the inquest jury's seventy-one recommendations was urging the establishment of a national sex offender registry. After five years of inaction by the federal government, Ontario announced in 1999 that it would pursue its own provincial sex offender registry. When I heard the announcement I went to my boss and said that I wanted the OPP to take the lead in getting the registry set up. I offered my services to head up the effort. What was more, I knew the registry would be a perfect fit with what we were currently doing in BSS. The government approved the OPP taking the lead in researching, developing, maintaining and managing the new registry as part of BSS.

As it neared the time to introduce the legislation, it was proposed to Jim and Anna that the sex offender registry be named

Christopher's Law. Jim later said, "I thought, 'No, no, you won't put Christopher's name on this. This was dealing with sex offenders. It was a sex offender who sexually assaulted and then murdered our son.' I didn't want to have his name on that legislation, but then Anna and I talked about it after and she wondered why I was having difficulty. She thought it would be a good legacy and that it would be significant to give some meaning to the work that we had done and for what Christopher had been through."

And so it was decided that Christopher's legacy would be much more than his horrible death. In 2001 Ontario proclaimed Bill 31, An Act in Memory of Christopher Stephenson, referred to as "Christopher's Law." Ontario was the first and only province in Canada to establish a sex offender registry and within a few years had one of the highest offender registration rates worldwide. Ontario Sex Offender Registry staff and I joined Jim and Anna in continuing to lobby the federal government, and Canada's National Sex Offender Registry was finally established in 2004.

Jim's favourite story to tell about his son was about the time when he and Anna were sitting around the kitchen table talking with Christopher and Amanda about what they wanted to be when they grew up. Jim said, "I told Christopher that when I was his age my teacher asked me what I wanted to be when I grew up and I told her I wanted to be a cowboy. Christopher kind of giggled, so I asked him, 'What do you want to be?' He said, 'I want to be a lawyer.' I asked him, 'Why do want to be a lawyer?' Christopher said, 'Because I want to make laws.'"

Christopher wasn't given a chance to be a lawyer, but the law that bears his name has gone a long way to save others from harm.

CHANGES AND CHANCES

"Maybe who we are isn't so much about what we do,
but rather what we're capable of when we least expect it."
Jodi Picoult, *My Sister's Keeper*

A LATE WINTER STORM HAD ROLLED INTO Ottawa over-night and it was still snowing in the morning when Trapper and I came out the front door of our downtown hotel. Bob was still sleeping and, as usual, I was on the early shift for dog walking, still wearing my pajamas underneath my winter parka and bare feet inside my snow boots. I pulled Trapper across Wellington Street and into the first open space in front of a government building we came to. There couldn't have been a worse location to be caught short of a poop bag—the snow-covered front lawn of the Supreme Court of Canada. But my violation of the poop-and-scoop law wasn't the only thing that weighed on my mind that day. I'd been kicking a bit of snow onto all my problems lately and they were just getting worse.

It was April 4, 2003, and Bob and I were in Ottawa as I was

receiving the Governor General's Order of Merit of the Police Forces medal from Adrienne Clarkson. The investiture invitation said I was in the top tenth of 1 percent of the members of police forces for my "exemplary contributions to establishing and promoting concepts in behavioural sciences, concepts that enhance public safety and victim assistance."[9] I was receiving a lot of accolades from police services and professional groups for my work and to now have my country recognize my service career was such an honour—but at the same time I was feeling a mounting sense of guilt and doubt.

Because the truth was, I didn't want to do this job anymore. In the course of my workday I'd be taking calls for assistance on

Receiving the Governor General's Order of Merit of the Police Forces medal from Adrienne Clarkson, 2003.

homicide, sexual assault and child abuse cases, and when I'd hang up the phone a wave of anxiety would surge up into my chest. Thankfully I had other extremely capable BSS staff that I could assign the cases to. The thought of looking at one more crime report or set of photographs or watching one more video-tape made me feel sick to my stomach. Shortly after I returned from Ottawa I stepped down as president of the ICIAF, not wanting to attend any conferences or meetings where these kinds of cases would be discussed. I'd never before experienced such mental and physical fatigue.

I didn't see a doctor about what I was experiencing. I'd been working in the business long enough to be able to diagnose myself. Over the years I had helped some of my own staff deal with stress-related health issues and I'd even recently collabo-rated with Peter Collins in setting up "Project Safeguard" to help those working in undercover assignments deal with the stress in their jobs. I knew what was causing the anxiety and fatigue and I knew what the solution was.

I told no one, not even Bob, about what was going on with me. Frankly, Bob and I weren't really talking about much of anything anymore. We'd drifted apart and neither of us seemed happy. I thought it might be just a phase and that we'd get through it. While it saddened me that we seemed to be going the way of so many other police marriages, we officially became another statistic when he moved out.

In 2004 I was selected as Police Leader of the Year by the Canadian Police Leadership Forum. It was another enormous hon-our, but again I didn't derive as much satisfaction from it as I felt I should have. Right after the announcement I went to my boss and told him I needed to get out of BSS. He was surprised but didn't ask any questions nor delay in getting me a new assignment.

Within a few weeks I was the director of Intelligence Bureau. I had zero background in intelligence work, other than passing along the odd piece of information to the bureau that I came across when I was working in uniform or undercover. Intelligence had over one hundred staff and I knew little about their work in antiterrorism probes, witness relocation, informant development or intelligence gathering. But the officers and support staff pitched in and got me up to speed. The best part was, even though some days I'd come to work not knowing what the hell I was doing, I felt exhilarated about my job again. I loved the new business I was in, and within weeks felt healthy again and back to my old self.

I attended many of my meetings with my counterparts from other agencies with one of my subject matter experts in tow. The often-long drives to different parts of the province gave me the opportunity to get to know them and their work and for them to get to know me. My predecessors were all male and most had either come up through the ranks or had at least some experience when they took over the director's position. My own internal intelligence-gathering efforts revealed that one of my managers had more than a little resistance to the idea of me being the new boss and was apparently quite vocal about it—except to my face of course.

One winter day I decided it would be good for me and this manager to take a road trip together. It didn't go particularly well. En route he told me how he and the other managers in the office were getting together in the near future for an office meeting and to do a little ice fishing. Apparently it was an annual event, apparently I wasn't invited and apparently I was supposed to pay for their getaway. Well, that wasn't happening. I countered with a story that I had already arranged a "me and the boys" office meeting at a hotel and spa. I told him that we would have our meetings during the day and I would be booking spa appointments for all of us in the evenings. He told me he didn't think the guys would like that. I told him they better get used to working for a woman. A period of silence followed and then I told him I was kidding. I'm not sure that he took the joke so well. On the way home, he filled up my unmarked police car with gas and topped up the engine coolant. The next time I was driving the car and needed to spray some washer fluid on my windshield, it squirted out engine coolant instead. Since we eventually ended up working fairly well together after the initial period, I will give him the benefit of the doubt that it was an honest mistake.

In 2006 a uniform position as the chief superintendent in charge of Investigation Support Bureau was advertised, so I threw my hat into the competition ring. I was familiar with the bureau commander job since it was the position that I reported to when I was manager of BSS. I was successful and became the first female commander of Investigation Support Bureau responsible for the specialty areas of forensic identification, electronic and physical surveillance, behavioural sciences, criminal investigations and a relatively new area of expertise, electronic crime.

The Electronic Crime Section (E-Crime) was my steepest

learning curve because I knew so little about it. I found out it was no longer as simple as police attending a crime scene, collecting evidence, interviewing witnesses and taking statements. New exploitive opportunities for cybercrimes were being created daily: superviruses; intellectual property fraud; attacks on wireless communications and storage systems; Internet-facilitated identity theft schemes; and online extortion. The crime business had gone global, rarely occurring in one jurisdiction and we were often dealing with multiple offenders residing in different locations around the world.

There were not only new challenges for front-line detectives, but also for my forensic electronic analysts. It seemed every criminal investigation the OPP did had some form of technology-based evidence seized. It was often crucial evidence of the crimes committed:

- Homicide investigators were able to locate the body of a missing child after the murderer's cellphone pings off a nearby telecommunications tower led them to the area where the child's remains were located.
- Drug investigators seized a cellphone from an arrested marijuana grower and discovered it contained a photograph of another large crop ready for harvest. A couple of clicks more on the phone and investigators had the GPS coordinates of the photograph and went on over to do a "meet-and-greet" with the harvesters.
- At the murder trial of a police officer shot and killed in the line of duty, a sampling of seized computer data was

presented to the jury. A stack of photocopied pages from various Internet sites demonstrated the killer's interest in weapons in general and especially in the five days prior to killing the officer. The stack was three inches high.

- In a domestic-terrorism investigation, 4.3 terabytes of data were seized as evidence of the crimes committed. Just one terabyte's worth of stacked paper would be 66,000 miles high.

Having to deal with the potential negative impact of having so much information, some of it being evidence of the crime, was a whole new management issue that I had never dealt with before. And since large segments of the public had minimal knowledge about how computers and the Internet really worked, there were inexhaustible opportunities for criminals to exploit. Particularly vulnerable were children. Police officers and civilian technology analysts were responding with limitless imagination and determination to make the Internet a safer place for kids.

One example of such a creative approach came from the founder of the Toronto Police Service Child Exploitation Section, Paul Gillespie. In 2006 Gillespie took the initiative to email Bill Gates asking for help in battling the online sexual exploitation of children. Microsoft responded with a partnership investment to co-create a new software package to assist in tracking online predators, valued at over $4 million.[10]

OPP e-crime programmer Trevor Fairchild developed an award-winning software package for use by child pornography investigators to categorize millions of photographs and movies seized in their investigations. The program was made available free to law enforcement and security agencies worldwide. A co-worker of Trevor's, programmer and analyst Joseph Versace, developed a software program that monitored peer-to-peer child pornography file sharing in cyberspace twenty-four hours a day, tracking all known images of child pornography being shared online.

And then there were people with good intentions who were using the Internet to try to find information to help family or friends or even strangers. Sometimes they didn't even know the people they were trying to help. The combined efforts of three web sleuths who'd never met would eventually solve a seventeen-year-old missing person's case.

Jen was a young woman from the Niagara, New York, area who was searching the Internet trying to find information about her uncle who'd been missing since 1993. Jen's uncle, Russell, or Rusty as they called him, hadn't been in touch with his family in over a decade.

Jen had vivid childhood memories of Rusty. "He was a quirky man with a big heart," she said. "Rusty was a hunter and one time when he was living with my grandmother she told him she would like to have a fresh turkey for Thanksgiving. Rusty brought home an actual live turkey from somewhere that he kept in the basement for two days. Damn did that thing make noise. I liked to pet it. Then it made an appearance on the table for Thanksgiving dinner. I believe that was the year I became a vegetarian."

Jen liked to remember the funny stories, but there was another side to her uncle. As Rusty grew older, his life started to spiral downward. He was plagued with mental health problems and was eventually diagnosed with schizophrenia and spent time in a hospital. His heavy drinking only exacerbated his illness.

Jen joined the US Armed Forces when she was nineteen and moved away. She heard through her family that Rusty got married and then divorced, was living by himself in a small apartment and barely surviving on his disability pension. He had associations with a local motorcycle gang, was abusing drugs as well as alcohol and had a criminal record.

Rusty was thirty-six when his mother died in the spring of 1992. A short time later he received a message that he was not included in her will, although it wasn't true—his mother had actually arranged for him to receive a monthly allotment managed by his sister and brother. Family members tried to notify Rusty, but he'd dropped out of sight, as he was often prone to do. It wasn't till more than a year later, in June 1993, that Rusty's social services caseworker officially reported him missing, advising that his mail was unclaimed and his social assistance cheques had not been cashed.

Jen's family didn't know what had happened to Rusty. "We didn't know if he was avoiding us or if perhaps because of some of his associations and involvement in criminal behaviour he might have been killed. We didn't know where to look. We felt so helpless."

In 2005, after a difficult marriage breakup, Jen was back living in the Niagara area, a single mother with two young children. She saw first-hand how hard it was for her mother to have a brother missing, and for the whole family not to know whether

Rusty was dead or alive. Jen searched hundreds of American Internet sites and missing persons' directories but found nothing. Some sites contacted her with offers of assistance, in some cases asking as much as a thousand dollars. Desperate to find answers for her family, Jen ended up being taken in by one—she was determined not to let it happen again.

In December 2005, Jen placed a short message about her uncle on the "I Care" message board, an interactive site for posting and commenting on cases relating to missing and unidentified persons, as well as unsolved homicides.[11] Using the alias "Sidhfaerie," Jen posted a message that her uncle was mentally ill, had red hair and that he was missing a pinky finger from a childhood accident. She requested that anyone with information contact Niagara Falls police.

Kim Peters, the manager of BSS's ViCLAS Unit, was aware of the frustrations people like Jen had when searching for their missing loved ones. He said, "The seeds of an idea started in 2005 when I was sitting in my carport one night smoking a cigar and thinking about a missing person's case that I was working on in ViCLAS. We had a lot of information in the ViCLAS database about missing persons but we didn't have a lot of unidentified human remains entered, especially the older ones. I decided to do some research to see how many missing persons and unidentified remains we had in Ontario. I found out there were about fifteen hundred people in Canada listed as missing on the CPIC [Canadian Police Information Centre] website but very few unidentified remains were on the system."

Kim knew from his experience in managing the ViCLAS Unit that a centralized database of violent crimes allowed his analysts to successfully search for information and link similar crimes. The same searchable-type database for missing persons and unidentified bodies could make links as well, especially if the information previously held only by police and coroners could be made electronically available for linkage analysis by the public.

Together with Ontario's Office of the Chief Coroner, BSS contributed staff and funding to research, develop and launch an analytical software program known as the Resolve Initiative. On May 6, 2006, the OPP announced the publicly accessible website, the first of its kind in Canada.[12]

Kim took on the additional responsibility of running the OPP's newly formed Missing Persons Unidentified Bodies (MPUB) Unit which was inputting all of the data and managing the program. Police and members of the public were able to conduct inquiries relating to persons' physical characteristics like height, weight, hair and eye colour. Search parameters included when and where they were last seen and distinctive features such as scars and tattoos. When the site went live, it had over three hundred cases entered in the system.

Media coverage of the OPP's website launch was crucial in making the public aware of this new tool. One person who was particularly intrigued was a young Toronto resident named Jordan. He was employed in the media industry but, as a hobby, spent many hours searching for missing people on the Internet. He began to peruse the cases on the OPP site in his spare time.

On several occasions Jordan contacted the MPUB Unit to pass on information he had turned up on the web. Jordan developed a reputation with those working in MPUB as a knowledgeable and reliable tipster. And there was one entry on the website that kept nagging at Jordan.

CASE #: 20060020

DATE FOUND: 5/15/1993

AGE (ESTIMATED): 35–50

GENDER: Male

RACE: Caucasian

HEIGHT: 165 cm: 5 ft 4 in

WEIGHT: 86 kg: 189 lbs

BUILD: Heavy-set

DENTAL: N/A

HAIR: Blond/red hair with tight waves, short at the front longer at the back, Red;

FACIAL HAIR: Moustache

EYES: Blue

UNIQUE FEATURES:

- Healed semi-circular scar on right knee approximately 13 cm long
- Missing small finger on left hand
- Metal plate in right clavicle with 6 screws
- Right thumb is short and fat
- Nicotine stains right index and middle fingers
- Tattoo of name "RUSTY" on chest

HABITS: N/A

CLOTHING:

- Pants, Jeans, Blue
- Socks, White, Wearing a double pair of white socks
- Shirt, T Shirt, White, Logo is a diamond shape with a skier and wording "No Guts, No Glory, from Whistler, BC"
- Belt, Brown, Silver coloured belt buckle with a picture of a bear on it
- Footwear, Running shoes, White, White with blue trim
- Sweater, White, Size Large, With brown and yellow transverse stripe across chest and arms, picture of a buffalo on upper left chest

PERSONAL EFFECTS:

- Green "Bic" lighter
- Black comb
- Vinyl change wallet

SUMMARY: The body of this adult male was found near a foot bridge at Rosedale Valley Road.

LOCATION FOUND: Toronto, Ontario

POLICE SERVICE: Toronto Police Service–51 Division

CONTACT US:

1-877-9FIND ME (1-877-934-6363) Toll Free in North America

opp.isb.resolve@ontario.ca

(705) 330-4144 for local or outside of North America or Crime Stoppers at 1-800-222-TIPS (8477)

Jordan knew he had seen that missing finger mentioned somewhere before. He went back and searched through the many missing person sites he had scanned in the past. He eventually made his way back to the "I Care" website and located the posting. He didn't want to communicate with the person openly on the site, so he set about searching to identify the alias, "Sidhfaerie," that was used in the original message. A Google search resulted in him finding a post on a US Armed Forces message board, with the same unique alias, as well as an email address.

In the early evening of February 21, 2008, Jen received Jordan's first message about her missing uncle, not through the "I Care" site, but directly to her email address. It read, "Hello. I'm not sure if I'm emailing the correct person or not so forgive me if this sounds a little strange. Are you "Sidhfaerie" from the icaremissing website?" Jen sent back, "Yes, I am Sidhfaerie . . . in search of Russell Pensyl from Lockport, NY."

Jen replied to Jordan's anonymous email by stating that she was unsure of his intentions and had no money to pay for information. She told him that she was the missing man's niece and wasn't even sure if her uncle would want to be found or even if he was still alive.

Jordan told her he understood her apprehension and was not interested in any payment for information. He explained how he'd discovered details of a man that was missing a pinky finger and that they matched the description of her uncle. He ended his message with, "I understand your trust concerns. Here I am a stranger, emailing you out of the blue and it looks weird. I really just want to help."

The two corresponded back and forth over the next several hours. With each piece of additional information she sent him,

Jordan realized that he was getting closer and closer to confirming the sad reality that this family's missing relative died in Toronto almost seventeen years earlier. Jen wanted to know where Jordan lived. He told her and said he would have a detective contact her by email.

The next morning an officer contacted Jen and directed her to the MPUB website. She was devastated with what she found but was ultimately grateful to Jordan for helping them find their loved one.

Ident was able to obtain fingerprints from the US and use them to positively confirm the dead man as Russell Pensyl. Jen was advised that, since her uncle Rusty remained unidentified for so long, he had been buried by Toronto Social Services on February 26, 2001, in a cemetery just north of the city. Jen looked up the burial location on the Internet and wrote one last message to Jordan, "The cemetery is so beautiful, and it would be a shame to disturb his final resting place. He should stay . . . And I thank you again for giving me a little faith in humanity back."

I later spoke with Jordan and he mentioned that it would have been nice if he and Jen could have met in person. I told him to leave it with me. When I talked to Jen by phone she was excited not only to accept my invitation to travel to Canada and meet Jordan and me, but also have an opportunity to visit her uncle's grave. I chose a restaurant for the three of us to meet for lunch in the north end of Toronto. The cemetery was just down the street.

Jen and I arrived first and were both laughing at one of her childhood stories of her uncle when Jordan arrived. He and Jen hugged one another like old friends. For the next few hours they shared stories about each other's families and reminisced about the night they met online. They both shared with me the struggles that families and friends have in trying to locate loved ones and the need for better systems and centralized databases to assist in their searches. They were pleased to hear what I could tell them on the progress of the federal government's initiative to establish a national missing persons' and unidentified remains database.

After lunch, Jen and Jordan said goodbye with promises to stay in touch. I had Jen follow me in her car to the cemetery and we located the area in which her uncle was buried. She became quite emotional and told me that she would like to spend some time alone. I told her I understood and gave her a small glass replica of a Canadian Inuit inukshuk as a gift to thank her for travelling to Canada and agreeing to meet with Jordan and me. On hearing that the stacked rocks were considered a symbol of hope and friendship, she said she would always keep it as a symbol of what Canadians did for her family.

BROKEN DREAMS

Not everyone knows how it feels to have your whole world ripped
out from under you in less than a day. No hugs, no "see you later,"
no goodbyes, just a part of my heart ripped out . . . My sister
was the only person I had to talk to, someone that felt what I felt,
cried when I cried, laughed when I laughed, and now I feel alone,
like the world is playing a sick trick on me . . .
—From the victim impact statement of thirteen-year-old Daryn Stafford,
brother of Tori Stafford

I ARRIVED IN WOODSTOCK on the evening of May 21, 2009, shortly after eleven o'clock. The town of 38,000 is about 150 kilometres west of Toronto in the heart of dairy farming country. Many of its blue-collar residents work at area automotive and supply companies. Like most towns' streets, there were lots of changeable-letter-board signs outside churches, stores and restaurants. But instead of inspirational gospel quotes, sale prices or special dinner features, for the last six weeks the signs had advertised nothing but hope for the safety of a little girl. The signs read, "Tori we love you," "Tori we are praying for you," and "Tori please come home safe." The evening I arrived in town the signs had all been changed again. They now expressed sorrow and support for the family of a little eight-year-old girl named Victoria ("Tori") Elizabeth Marie Stafford, now believed to be dead.

I was so taken with the displays that I didn't go straight to the hotel that CIB DI Bill Renton and other OPP detectives had filled to capacity over the last six weeks. Instead I felt compelled to drive around town to look at more of the signs. Their messages demonstrated such profound community solidarity. It appeared as though the whole town was in mourning. When I finally checked in to the hotel, I left a message for Bill to meet me for breakfast the next morning.

My bureau had been reorganized in recent months and now CIB reported to me. I wanted to get Bill's first-hand update on the case and details about his recent two arrests. I was also anxious to meet with his team. After twenty years of being involved in these types of cases and knowing how they could affect you on a personal level, I wanted them to know that I not only appreciated their work but also cared about their well-being. I knew they'd had high hopes that their dedication and hard work would find Tori and bring her home. The last few days would have been tough for them.

I was already familiar with the details of Tori's abduction as I'd gotten back into doing some profiling again after being away from it for a couple of years—taking some time away and doing other work had been just what I'd needed. There'd been a BSS team on the ground in Woodstock since Tori first went missing and they'd talked to me on the phone, as well as met with me back up in Orillia to get my opinion on a couple of aspects of the case. I'd even arranged for some of my profiling colleagues, including the FBI's Ken Lanning from Quantico, to come up and take a look at the case, but that meeting was cancelled at the last minute with news of the arrests.

On the afternoon of April 8, Tori, a Grade 3 student, was abducted as she walked away from her school on her way home. The only concrete evidence in the investigation was what happened seconds after she exited the school building. It was a grainy piece of security video footage shot from a high school adjacent to Tori's school. The footage showed her walking away with what appeared to be a woman wearing a light-coloured coat. Tori was wearing a hooded *Hannah Montana* shirt bearing the caption "A Girl Can Dream" and a denim skirt. She was also wearing a pair of butterfly earrings that her mother had lent to her that morning.

Since her disappearance, Tori's mother, Tara McDonald, held almost daily press briefings from the front porch of her home to a number of media outlets. Tori's abduction was also featured on an episode of *America's Most Wanted*. Each day Tara pleaded for the safe return of her daughter and for anyone who had information to come forward. She often shared her only daughter's handwritten notes, drawings and personal belongings as she told stories about Tori's home and school life. Her ex-husband and Tori's father, Rodney Stafford, was often present for the porch-stoop media scrums as well. Despite a less than amicable split back in 2002, after four years of marriage, they did their best to appear aligned in their mission to bring their daughter home. On several occasions their then eleven-year-old son, Daryn, was present with them. Their public appearances garnered considerable interest from the public, and at the same time kept the story of Tori's abduction in the media forefront.

Eight days after Tori's abduction, the OPP joined forces with the original investigating agency, Oxford County Police Service. The number of tips coming in on the case and the daily expanding scope of the searches for Tori were beyond the capabilities of the small city police service. Police Chief Ron Fraser was appreciative of the help. The number of investigators jumped from fifteen to more than a hundred within the first week.

Bill Renton was from the area and had assisted the small community police service in another murder investigation in the recent past. His biggest issue was the sheer volume of the case. He immediately set up the PowerCase computer software management system in use by all Ontario police services. The software provided for centralized data storage, evidence management and assignment tracking, and a host of other features that investigators required. Three detectives were assigned full-time just to read the seventy-five to a hundred tips received each day and prioritize them.

The OPP sent equipment and officers from around the province to Woodstock to assist in the search for Tori and the investigation into her abduction. In the months of April and May, more than 63,000 people accessed the MPUB website where Tori's abduction/missing person case was posted. The community also became actively involved in assisting in the many searches and rallies held in support of Tori's family. Many town residents would come up to the unfamiliar "suits" in their streets, coffee shops and restaurants and, without even asking who they were, thank the detectives for their efforts.

One of the "suits" was Jim Smyth, the third trained OPP criminal profiler, now working as a forensic polygraph examiner. He was in town conducting polygraph examinations and interviews on prioritized persons of interest. Four days after Tori disappeared police had received a tip from her mother, and an officer subsequently paid a visit to eighteen-year-old Terri-Lynne McClintic to talk to her—as well as take the opportunity to arrest her on an outstanding warrant. McClintic seemed to be forthright and have reasonable answers for all of his questions about Tori's disappearance. Everything changed when police got a tip about McClintic's boyfriend, twenty-eight-year-old Michael Rafferty, who didn't answer officers' questions about Tori's disappearance so well and came off as evasive.

Investigators wanted Jim to take a second harder look at McClintic and offer her a polygraph. She took the test, but it came out inconclusive. She was a good liar, but only initially. When Jim went into interview mode, McClintic's previously stable house of cards soon came tumbling down and she confessed to her involvement in Tori's abduction and murder. She revealed that the girl had been murdered within hours of her being taken. She also implicated Rafferty, who was also charged with first-degree murder, along with kidnapping and sexual assault causing bodily harm.

That night Bill brought together about forty of his team, detectives and civilian support staff to share the break in their case. Everyone was devastated. He then went to tell Tori's parents and their families himself.

The morning I met Bill for breakfast in Woodstock, I found him waiting for me alone at a table in an empty section of the hotel restaurant. He looked exhausted. Dave Cardwell, the director of CIB, joined us a short time later and the three of us drove over to the project offices set up in an empty warehouse. Bill had civilians and officers gather together to hear Dave and me acknowledge their work and offer our support. I found myself saying many of the same things that I'd heard Ken Lanning say to the police on the Michael Dunahee case almost two decades earlier. Despite what had happened, these men and women had done everything they could to bring Tori home. We would continue our search for Tori, as British Columbia was still searching for Michael. There was one big difference. We had two people in custody who knew where Tori was.

The investigation's focus was preparing the criminal prosecution case against McClintic and Rafferty and finding Tori's remains. Rafferty was uncooperative with police, but Jim and several other officers spent considerable time with McClintic in the days after her arrest. Using a police helicopter in the air and unmarked cruiser on the ground, Jim tried to work with her to re-create the route she and Rafferty had followed in his car after they took Tori. She gave a very detailed description of a side road just off a main concession road, a house and a lane through a field. Jim believed she was telling him the truth in her descriptions, but they couldn't identify the complete route she and Rafferty took, nor could they find the final place where Tori was brutally attacked, murdered and her body disposed of.

OPP Emergency Response Team members (ERT) from across Ontario continued with search efforts throughout the summer. They were assisted by other OPP and area police services and many members of the public who came out just wanting to help the family in some small way. At one point some officers were assigned to look for possible evidence that had been disposed of and they worked in a landfill site for thirty-one days. Day after day they went through the garbage, without complaint—and unfortunately without success.

On Friday, July 17, Bill received information that Rafferty used his mobile phone within several hours after Tori's abduction and some of his calls had pinged off a tower in the town of Mount Forest. That location was outside the perimeter of the searches that had been completed up until that time. Bill decided that, rather than call searchers in to work over the weekend, he would give them some well-deserved time off. Bill asked Jim to work the weekend and get prepared for the expanded search the following week.

Like so many others, Jim hadn't had many nights at home, so late Saturday afternoon he decided to make the two-hour drive home to attend a family function that evening. He got up early on Sunday morning to head back to Woodstock. When driving down Highway 400 Jim decided to cut off and take a side road over to take a look at the area they would be searching that week.

He zigzagged along country roads as he worked his way south. Suddenly he came upon an area that looked just as McClintic had described several months earlier. He drove down the lane and saw a pile of rocks up ahead, again just as she'd said. Jim parked a ways back from the rocks and got out of his car. His first breath was confirmation. He'd smelled that odour before.

I was notified and called Jim's cellphone right away. His voice was shaky when he answered. The adrenalin was obviously still flowing. He was still at the scene.

"Are you sure, Jim?" I asked.

"Yeah, I'm sure," he said.

Jim had found Tori 103 days after her abduction. She was positively identified at autopsy through her dental records. She had been raped and savagely beaten. Her cause of death was multiple blunt impact injuries.

I worried about my officers, even the ones that I knew well like Jim, and how they would cope with situations like these. Families often provided the strongest support. Jim's father was a retired senior officer with York Regional Police. He and Jim's mother knew he was working on Tori's abduction but that was all, since Jim never spoke about his work. His dad later told me, "Jim's mother had said to him, 'Jim, you find that little girl and bring her home.' The day they had it on the news that a lone OPP officer found her body they didn't say who it was. But his mother just said, 'That's Jim.' I was thinking the same thing. Later we found out it *was* him, not through Jim, but from media reports. We knew what he was going through at work, but we didn't need to know the details. He was raised in a police family and knows there is always an umbrella overtop of him."

Sometimes a family's umbrella held overhead isn't enough to fend off the torrent of emotions felt by uniform and civilian staff working under these circumstances. The day after Tori's body was discovered I again went to the warehouse offices in Woodstock. This time OPP commissioner Julian Fantino was with me. We knew there was nothing we could really say to ease the emotion of the situation. Like my last visit, I hoped at least our words and physical presence demonstrated our support.

That day, critical incident debriefing teams were with us too. I knew the value of people being able to openly discuss the emotional and physical impact and share with each other what they were experiencing. At that time the sessions were most often led by our own force psychologist, assisted by police officers who had been through traumatic incidents themselves.

On July 31 many of those working on the case attended Tori's funeral.

McClintic pleaded guilty to the first-degree murder of Tori and was sentenced to twenty-five years in prison. After a publication ban was lifted, the public were advised of the Agreed Statement of Facts read after her plea. It confirmed that she was the woman in the light-coloured jacket in the videotape. She had started a conversation about dogs with Tori when she met her outside the school. She lured her to a nearby car, driven by Rafferty, telling her there was a puppy inside.

Following a ten-week judge-and-jury trial in the nearby city of London, Rafferty was convicted of kidnapping, sexual assault causing bodily harm and first-degree murder. He was sentenced to life in prison with no chance of parole for twenty-five years.

Despite the outcome, the team working on this case had a lot to be proud of. They successfully concluded an investigation that involved over 900 officers from different police agencies, 50 civilians, 7,500 officer reports, 2,200 civilian statements, 5,500 tips followed up and hundreds of hours of videotape footage viewed. Search teams covered 18,144 kilometres of territory. Unfortunately none of their hard work, or the hopes and prayers of millions of people, could bring Tori home alive.

THE FINAL TRIBUTE

"Perseverance is more prevailing than violence; and many things
which cannot be overcome when they are together,
yield themselves up when taken little by little."
—Plutarch (AD 46–AD 120)

I KNEW KEN LEPPERT BY REPUTATION before I ever met him. One of the first CIB investigations he'd been assigned was a cold case that many thought would never be solved. Allen and Margaret Campbell had gone missing from their cottage on Trout Lake near North Bay on May 29, 1956. They were presumed to have drowned but there was never any proof. Media attention given to the fiftieth anniversary of their disappearance managed to elicit new information about where they were last seen on the lake in their boat. Using recently developed side scanning sonar technology to examine the bottom of the lake, Ken and his team searched the new area—and found the couple in twenty-five metres of water. As suspected, their deaths were from drowning. So Ken started off his CIB career with a bang by solving the fifty-year-old case.

A couple of years later, when Ken was in Orillia for a meeting, he stopped by my office to talk to me. By this time we'd met a couple of times but I didn't know him that well. It was late in the afternoon and I was catching up on some paperwork before heading home when he appeared at my doorway.

"Have you got a minute?"

"Sure. Come on in and have a seat. What's up?"

"I just finished a brain storming session with UHIT [Unsolved Homicide Investigation Team]. I'd like to talk to you about Kirkland Lake."

As soon as he mentioned Kirkland Lake I knew what he was talking about. It was never a "whodunit," but rather a "how do we get him." It was the oldest missing persons' case I'd ever approved for CIB to reinvestigate and had already been revisited in 1986, 1991 and again starting in 2006.

Back in 1970 twelve-year-old Katherine May Wilson went missing just outside Kirkland Lake, about six hundred kilometres north of Toronto. She was believed to have been abducted and presumed murdered. We were confident Kathy's second cousin on her father's side, Barry Manion, was responsible. There was just never enough evidence to lay charges against him.

Kathy went missing from Harvey Kirkland, just outside the Kirkland Lake town limit. It was a community of about seventy to eighty residents living in shanty-type homes, few of which had running water or indoor toilets. For many, raising their own animals, hunting and fishing, along with what they could grow in their own gardens, was what put food on the table.

Kathy's father, Garnet, was a diamond driller at Adams Mine. Her mother, Aline, had got as far as Grade 5 in school and was married at fifteen. Aline started having children when she was eighteen and had five by the time she was twenty-two. In 1970 Kathy was the oldest at twelve. Karen and Bobby were next. Eight-year-old Aline, nicknamed "Pee Wee," was the youngest. Their brother, Kenneth, died at three months of age from sudden infant death syndrome.

On Tuesday, October 20, 1970, the simple life of the Wilson family changed forever. The kids all left in the morning to walk one and a half kilometres into town to school. Aline told her husband that she wanted to go into town to pick up her government baby bonus cheque at the post office. Garnet persuaded her to go partridge hunting with him instead. They spent the early part of the day hunting and then Garnet went in to work the afternoon shift at the nearby mine. Aline didn't have a chance to go into town before the children got home from school.

Kathy's favourite pastime after school was riding her neighbour's horses but that day she came straight home, anxious to know if her mother had picked up the cheque, since Kathy had been promised a new pair of shoes. Her mother told her she hadn't picked it up yet and asked Kathy to walk back into town to the post office to get it and pick up a few groceries as well.

Kathy asked her little sister Pee Wee to come with her but she didn't want to. Kathy walked into town alone, picked up the cheque at the post office and then walked to a small grocery store. She telephoned her mother from there at about 5:00 p.m., wanting to know if she could buy a pop and a snack. She was told she could have one or the other. It was the last time Aline spoke to her daughter.

After the call, Aline told Pee Wee and her older sister Karen to go meet Kathy. As the girls were walking on Harvey Kirkland Road toward town, they met Manion driving his boss's pickup truck with "Brown's Auto Supply" painted on the side. At the time he was twenty-two years old, married with a three-year-old son and infant daughter and lived in town. He stopped and asked the girls if Kathy was still living at home and they told him she was.

The girls continued on into town but couldn't find Kathy and started back home. (It was later learned that Kathy stopped for a few minutes at a friend's home to share a bag of Cheezies and missed running into her sisters when they were coming into town.) Karen and Pee Wee were on Harvey Kirkland Road when the same pickup truck drove toward them again, speeding up as it got closer. Pee Wee lost her footing on the road and fell as it went by them, but Karen clearly saw Kathy on the passenger's side. Manion was driving and appeared to be pushing Kathy's head down. Karen made eye contact with Kathy as they drove by and then the pickup sped out of sight toward town.

The girls ran home and told their mother what they saw. Aline walked up the road toward town to look for Kathy herself. Finding no sign of her, she returned home. As time passed, panic set in and she called Garnet at work and then called the police. Garnet was home by the time the OPP came to the house. Karen told the officer what she had seen and he realized the incident was not in OPP jurisdiction—Harvey Kirkland Road was in

Teck Township and therefore the Teck Township Police Department were responsible for it. The Wilsons' home was in Lebel Township and under the jurisdiction of the Kirkland Lake OPP. The OPP officer left the Wilsons and went to the Teck police office and gave them what information he had. A Teck officer completed a missing person report including that Kathy was four foot nine, had dark curly hair, weighed just over a hundred pounds and the description of what she was wearing. Police went to Manion's residence later in the evening and told him Kathy was missing but Manion made no mention of seeing the girls earlier in the day. The officer talked to him for only a few minutes and then left.

The next morning Manion was driving on Highway 11 outside of Kirkland Lake in the same pickup and was involved in a serious single-car accident. When the police were again able to question him about Kathy's disappearance, he denied any knowledge of her whereabouts or ever having her in his pickup the day she went missing. Apparently the police believed him and not Kathy's sisters, as the police never spoke to Manion again and he moved away not long after.

Over the next several days vital time was wasted debating jurisdictional issues between the two police departments. The OPP detachment was also dealing with a fatal motor car accident and monitoring the nearby Quebec border during the infamous FLQ crisis. Meanwhile, in Kirkland Lake, a little girl was still missing and little investigating was being done.

Searches were conducted by the police with the help of many area residents, including some of Mr. Wilson's workmates at the mine who got paid leave to help. Meanwhile Pee Wee and the rest of her family walked the fields and through the bush surrounding Harvey Kirkland searching for Kathy.

Kathy's disappearance ended up being investigated jointly by the two neighbouring police agencies. Weeks turned into months and then years. All the while, the Wilsons were confident that Manion took their daughter but never challenged the inaction of the police. What Karen and Pee Wee Wilson told police they saw and who they spoke to while walking into town that day in 1970 was never formally documented in any police report. The information, scribbled on some rough notes and stored in a banker's box, wasn't found until a 1986 cold-case file review.

Garnet and Aline eventually separated and divorced. Their son, Bobby, died in 1992 and Garnet passed away in 2002. Over the years people contacted Aline with information about her daughter, but when the police interviewed them they'd deny what they'd said to Aline. She thought they were looking for attention, but always let the police know just in case. A private investigator once contacted her advising he had somebody that had seen Kathy. She had him do some work but soon realized that every time he would call her with new information it was right before he was due more money. Aline ended up having to sell her home to pay him off.

In 2006, when Ken Leppert transferred to CIB, he was already familiar with the still-unsolved case and asked that it be assigned to him. Despite previously unsuccessful re-investigations, Ken was convinced that the case could still be solved. He said, "The reality was two different forces kept passing the buck. No one wanted to take responsibility. There seemed to be no ownership of the case and a lack of accountability all around. The two girls had seen who had taken their sister. It's like no one believed the girls or just didn't care." Ken wanted the OPP to try harder.

Ken and UHIT discussed a number of strategies that hadn't been attempted before and the fourth-round investigation proposal was approved by me. The last hurdle was to get OPP deputy commissioner Vince Hawkes to approve it.

The bosses in the "Ivory Tower" or "Puzzle Palace," as the boots on the street called headquarters, were often painted with broad brushes of criticism. According to some, we were supposedly too far removed from the real world of policing and therefore incapable of making good decisions. I have to admit I'd thrown a few darts myself earlier in my career, but as I made my way up the ladder I learned that bureaucracy had a playbook. You needed to know the rules and how to make them work to your advantage. Some days getting in to see Vince to get something approved was like taking a number in a Saturday morning deli line. I was usually queued up with suits in front and back of me, all with the same goal of getting the purse strings loosened in their favour for terrorism, organized crime or whatever mayhem they thought more important than mine.

You couldn't tag Vince with having his head in the clouds. He was a twenty-five-year veteran in charge of all of our technical and specialized investigative services, as well as the major case management program. He'd worked his way up through Ident to become the OPP's first bloodstain pattern analyst. He had an international reputation and court-recognized expertise. (He became the fourteenth commissioner of the OPP in 2014.)

I certainly knew I wouldn't get funding for a case that was thirty-six years old unless Vince was convinced it could be solved. He required little persuasion on this one and Ken was designated as the team commander of "Project Tribute."

Ken went to see Aline and her daughters in Kirkland Lake to tell them about the re-investigation. He said, "The Wilson family had been let down before. I didn't want to give them false hope. I listened to their concerns. I couldn't defend how they had been treated in the past so just apologized for it. Today this case would be investigated very differently. But it had happened in 1970. It was what it was."

Ken assigned a born-and-raised Kirkland Lake officer, Yvan Godin, as the lead investigator on the case. Josée Sabourin, from the neighbouring South Porcupine detachment, would look after file coordination. Keeping everything organized in a thirty-six-year-old case may not be the most exciting task, but it was one of the most important, and Josée was up for it.

Yvan and Josée found that virtually no officer notes were available from the initial investigation and no formal statements had been taken. The only documents available were police reports containing few details. Files from the more recent re-investigations contained notes from interviews but the two of them could see that witness memories were fading and there were discrepancies each time they were re-interviewed, which could be problematic in court. Some witnesses were now quite elderly so they needed to be videotaped and swear their statements under oath in case they died—not an easy topic to broach with a witness.

Civilian administrative assistant Karen Marshall had worked on the 1986 and 1991 re-investigations and she was back again. Karen and Josée worked together to input and update all information being gathered by the team, yielding a clear chronology of events and timeline for the October 20, 1970, activities of Kathy and her cousin. A total of twenty-six people had seen Kathy walking into town or on her way back home. Twelve people witnessed Manion in the same area that Kathy was walking around the time she went missing. Some of the witnesses were only now being interviewed for the first time.

Doug Bradley, a teenager in Kirkland Lake at the time that Kathy went missing, was the last addition to the team. He too had been involved in earlier investigations. He said, "Policing was done differently back then. You weren't hired in this town as a police officer on your ability but rather your size. You were given a uniform to wear and you wore it whether it fit you or not. In the early 70s there was no police training or police college. There were no police procedures or investigative manuals. There was no training whatsoever. Even though the officers were likely doing the best they could, this investigation was way beyond their ability back in the 70s. The way we do business today, Manion would have been locked up in the first day or two." Doug also had a special advantage: he knew Manion personally, having worked with him at the car dealership in Kirkland Lake in the late 60s.

————

When Ken came into my office that day and sat down, he seemed a bit nervous. He told me that he and the Project Tribute team had been brainstorming about strategies to bring the crime to the forefront of Manion's mind again. They were considering making a confrontational approach on him. Manion was twenty-two at the time of Kathy's disappearance and was now almost sixty.

Ken said, "We'd like to orchestrate someone to go face to face with him in a public place. The confrontation hopefully would embarrass him. It would also signal that we are still on the case and that we know he is the one that killed Kathy. He needs to know that we are not going to give up this investigation."

Ken shifted in his chair across from me and continued, "We'd like to do the confrontation with someone similar in age to Manion."

Now I knew where this conversation was going.

"Oh, so you're looking for an old undercover broad like me?"

Ken hesitated, "Well, it would be nice to have someone with your experience . . . and those are your words not mine."

Ken had a reputation for being a strategic investigator. Having a boss directly involved in the investigation could be helpful in keeping resources focused on his case. I didn't care—I was thrilled with the potential of returning to an era in my career I'd left over twenty years ago, no matter how small the role.

Ken left my office that afternoon with my commitment that I would do whatever he and his team wanted me to do.

Over two years a variety of investigative strategies were used to slowly draw Manion out of his quiet and comfortable lifestyle.

He was living common-law with a woman in London, Ontario, and again working at a car dealership. It was uncovered in one of the earlier re-investigations that he'd molested his two young nieces in the 1980s. He was convicted and received a two-year jail sentence. His two grown children, along with other family members and close acquaintances, were all interviewed again. Yvan and Doug told them that the investigation was finally coming to an end and that an arrest would be made in the near future. It wasn't a concern if what they said leaked back to Manion—it would be good to have him feel anxious and nervous about what was in store for him.

OPP criminal profilers Jim Van Allen, Ed Chafe and Karen Arney, along with forensic psychiatrist Peter Collins, participated in a number of round-table sessions and provided investigative suggestions in consideration of Manion's personality and anticipated psychological state. The ultimate goal was to have him in a state of mind conducive to confessing to Kathy's abduction. It was eventually decided that rather than do anything undercover it would be better for me to have a confrontation with Manion that was openly tied to the investigation. Gene Larocque was retired from Kirkland Lake OPP and part of the team that looked at the case in 1991. He was easily convinced to come back to work and be my partner in the confrontation. It was expected that Manion would immediately recognize Gene and likely assume I was his wife. We set it up that Gene and I would run into Manion in a Kingston-area casino where we knew he was meeting friends. It would be almost to the day of the thirty-eighth anniversary of Kathy's disappearance.

Gene and I met for the first time when we drove together from Orillia to Kingston. We scripted out some lines on our way and ran them by Ken who was waiting for us at our hotel when we arrived. He was good with the script and told us he'd also decided to have a plainclothes male and female officer, both whom I knew, sit near Manion in the restaurant to be our cover team.

A few hours later we got word that Manion was in the restaurant and our cover officers were in place. Back in my days as a UC I'd worked on all sorts of targets, from street hoods to outlaw biker gangs and there'd been some nerve-racking experiences. This one was a cake walk in comparison, but this time things were turned around because all of the investigative and surveillance team members standing by worked for me.

Gene and I went into the casino and found our way to the restaurant. Manion was ensconced in a corner booth table and our cover officers were sitting all in place. Gene and I sat at a table facing Manion and could see he was deep in conversation with his friends. He hadn't taken any notice of Gene or me coming in. I suggested to Gene we just go ahead over to him right away.

I followed Gene to his table. Gene was making it look like he wanted me to go sit back down. He kept telling me to stay back but I continued to follow him over to the table saying in a loud voice, "I'd like to say something to him."

Gene stopped in front of the table with me trying to get around him and get closer to Manion. When Manion looked up you could tell he recognized Gene right away.

Gene said, "I am surprised to see you here. Do you realize its thirty-eight years since Kathy Wilson disappeared . . . almost to the day."

He glared at Gene and said, "I don't remember."

Gene said, "I told you it wouldn't go away. The OPP will not let this go."

I leaned in over Gene's shoulder, crying and yelling at Manion. "You know what? You know what you should do? You should let that family put that little girl to rest."

Gene turned me around and was pushing me back away from the table. I then yelled over my shoulder, "You know what? The only justice would be if you would've died in that accident the next day."

Manion stood up and started looking around and yelling, "Security! Security!"

Gene and I hustled back to our table, grabbed our coats and left. The whole thing lasted all of about twenty seconds. Gene was laughing when we came out of the casino, complimenting me on my rant. They may not have been Academy Award–winning performances, but we both agreed it went according to plan and it felt good. A clear message was sent to Manion that even thirty-eight years later the OPP was still on the case.

When it came time to arrest Manion, Ken selected Josée to assist Yvan. I wasn't surprised. For the last several years she had worked tirelessly behind the scenes. Many of the investigative meetings were in southern Ontario and Josée would often leave home at three o'clock in the morning and drive more than nine hours to a meeting in southern Ontario that would start in the afternoon. On January 6, 2009, Yvan and Josée went to the car dealership where Manion worked and arrested him for abducting Kathy. They took him straight to the London OPP detachment.

Polygraph examiner Jim Smyth had been brought in from headquarters to interview Manion and was standing by. After getting Terri-Lynne McClintic's confession in the Tori Stafford case, Jim was considered one of the top police interviewers in the country. Over the next several hours, Ken and the team watched on closed-circuit TV as Jim tried to work his charms on Manion—but they didn't work so well this time. After several hours Manion wasn't denying any of Jim's accusations, but he wasn't admitting to anything either. It was the bottom of the ninth and Manion was shutting down. The opening pitcher had done what he could, but he needed a relief closer. Doug Bradley, watching from the monitoring room next door, volunteered to step onto the mound.

Manion recognized Doug as soon as he came into the interview room and seemed almost relieved to see him. Doug used a lower-key approach than Jim, slowly warming up to Manion with talk of their shared roots in Kirkland Lake. They reminisced about their time together as young men working at the car dealership and about the former co-workers and friends they once had in common.

After the pleasantries were over, Doug told Manion he'd been watching Jim and him talk for the last several hours and reiterated the evidence they had against him. Doug told him, "This is never going to go away," but Manion continued to deny any involvement.

Then Doug told Manion of his visits to his kids and encouraged him to do the right thing for them if not himself. Doug told him how his family was aware of what was happening right then. His son, who also lived in London, had called the detachment for information, having received word of his father's arrest. He told Manion his family was waiting, as was the Wilson family, to hear the outcome of their conversation. Doug played on Manion's ego and accentuated the control that Manion had over his own future. Doug told him, "It takes a big man to step up to the plate on this. You are the only one to give the family a proper burial. Give them back their daughter. Put the Wilsons at peace. Do the right thing."

Manion had been staring at the floor and suddenly looked up at Doug and said, "I want to speak with my son. This will be resolved after I talk to my son. And I want to talk to you after." After a couple of seconds he added, "I am relating to you. However you guys do it, you do it well."

As Doug got up to leave the room, Manion stood up and reached for Doug's hand and shook it. He said, "Make your phone call to Aline Wilson. I will make full disclosure."

Josée had been in the monitoring room all evening. "The whole team was in this small room, shoulder to shoulder, with me doing my best to type the conversation between the two of them as it was occurring. You could feel the energy in the room and the anticipation. Everyone was discussing different strategies to try next. Then when he said, 'I want to speak with my son,' the room went totally quiet."

Manion's son came to the detachment, and after a short

conversation with him, Manion gave Doug all the details of what happened, including that he had been molesting Kathy since she was eleven. He said he was angry and mad at the world the day it happened. He was on Harvey Kirkland Road, driving back and forth, looking for Kathy. After he picked her up, he was driving back to Kirkland Lake and saw her sisters on the road. He admitted trying to push Kathy's head down below the pickup truck's dash so they wouldn't see her. When Kathy found out she wasn't getting just a ride home from him as he'd offered, she got upset and kept asking him to take her home. He instead took her to a secluded area on the other side of town near Dorothy Lake. He parked the truck and tried to assault her. She fought him off, saying she wanted to go home and was going to tell her mother and father. She bolted from the truck and he chased after her. When he caught her, he strangled her. He retrieved the groceries that Kathy had with her in the pickup truck and left them beside her body. He covered her with tree branches and drove away. He told Doug he would go back to Kirkland Lake and show him where he left her body. He ended his statement with, "She did everything right and I did everything wrong."

After the confession, when Doug again got up to leave the room, Manion reached for his hand and shook it. "I feel good about this," he said. "Thanks for being who you are, not that your buddy didn't set you up good. I will praise you guys. You guys do a good job with respect and kindness. It was time to take ownership. Thanks, Bud."

Before they called it a night, Jim Smyth returned to the interview room to ask Manion what the key was to his confession.

Like anyone, Jim was interested in getting feedback on his craft. Manion said, "You got through to me. I kept trying to close you out, but you made me take stock of myself. You weren't ever going to go away."

I later congratulated Doug about keeping his cool during Manion's confession. He said, "That interview was just the way I have been doing business for my entire police career. The last thing that I wanted to show was disgust or revulsion. I knew we were close and I didn't want to lose him. The wrong word, expression or gesture could have just shut him right down. The impact the investigation was having on his family was definitely the tipping point. These re-investigations were rearing their heads every ten years or so. We'd go back to his kids each time and tell them. His kids were good kids, and they just wanted this thing to come to an end. I meant what I said to him that it would take a big man to cross that bridge. He could have taken it [the truth] to the grave with him."

In the early hours of January 7, thirty-nine years after Katherine May Wilson went missing, the only suspect in her disappearance was formally charged with her abduction and murder. Project Tribute, equipped with all of the necessary investigative tools and resources, was able to solve the case.

Yvan and Doug arranged to fly Manion up to Kirkland Lake the next morning but the weather didn't cooperate, with a snowstorm delaying their departure until late in the day. They arrived in Kirkland Lake in the evening and had lost daylight and any opportunity to search that day.

The next morning, with the temperature at -23 degrees Celsius,

Manion was escorted through town, retracing the route he took after he abducted Kathy. He and the officers travelled twelve kilometres north of Kirkland Lake into the area of Dorothy Lake where they then had to transfer to snowmobiles because of the snowfall. Given his emotional reaction to returning to the area for the first time since he'd murdered Kathy, and the area's consistency with his earlier descriptions, they were confident Manion was telling the truth that this was where he had killed Kathy. They recorded the GPS coordinates. They would have to wait until the spring thaw to search for Kathy's remains. It was unlikely that anything would be found, but they needed to at least try.

Ken met with the Wilsons at the detachment later that day when they got back to Kirkland Lake. Ken said, "I can remember Aline getting up and she was crying. She is a woman who has been through a lot in her life. She had been very averse to the police, as had the two sisters, and rightfully so. Every bit of animosity toward the police was completely justified. She got up and thanked us, hugged all of us and said through tears, 'Thank you. Now I can die in peace knowing what happened to my daughter.'"

Manion's lawyer advised the court that his client wished to plead guilty to the 1970 charge of non-capital murder. A March 11, 2009, court date was set at the courthouse in Haileybury. Manion entered his guilty plea, and an agreed-upon statement regarding the crime was read. He was given the maximum sentence of life imprisonment. Kathy's family was then given the opportunity to read a victim-impact statement.

Pee Wee and Karen went to the front of the court and stood in the witness box together. Pee Wee told an emotionally powerful and compelling story of the far-reaching effects Kathy's abduction and murder had on her family. The room remained silent when they stepped out of the box to return to their seats. As they walked past Manion he said, "Sorry." Karen turned and looked straight at him and said, "Fuck you," and continued on. Those were the only words anyone in the Wilson family ever spoke to him after Kathy went missing. One officer later told me, "That was the most eloquent 'fuck you' I have ever heard in my career. The judge heard it, everybody heard it, and nobody said a word. Everybody sat back and thought, 'If there was a time that you are ever entitled to say that, that was it.'"

After court Manion was taken to the Monteith Jail several hours away. Two days later, at about 5:00 a.m. on Friday the thirteenth, Manion was found dead, hanging on his cell door in Cellblock C. A mandatory coroner's inquest was held and the five-person jury determined his death was a suicide.

In the spring Ken kept calling up to the detachment to check on the snow and finally got word in early May that it was gone. Ken submitted one last funding request for Project Tribute to bring in archeologists and grid-search the wooded area. Nobody batted an eye about signing off on the request. This was all about doing the right thing by the Wilson family.

Two mobile command posts were set up and equipment moved in. Experts and student volunteers from Wilfrid Laurier University and the University of Toronto were joined by a bone specialist with Ontario's Office of the Fire Marshal. They searched from May 23 to June 12. Some days there were more than forty people on site. Aline, Karen and Pee Wee were there with the searchers just about every day, bringing with them the traditional offerings of Canadians' gratitude: Tim Hortons coffees and Timbits. Unfortunately, the search came up with nothing of Kathy's remains.

I eventually went up to Kirkland Lake to meet with the Wilson family. As I drove north on Highway 11, north of North Bay, I noticed a large billboard off to the right with the picture of a young teenaged girl whom I recognized immediately. In 1996 fifteen-year-old Melanie Ethier disappeared from the nearby town of New Liskeard. She was last seen when she'd left a friend's place around 2:00 a.m. to walk home. It was assumed that she hadn't left the area voluntarily. I'd assigned Jim Van Allen to profile the case and he consulted with me on it. But all of the resources of New Liskeard Police Service and the OPP had failed to uncover any trace of her in the last fifteen years. Her smiling school picture on the billboard had a caption underneath, "You know what happened to me . . . so why don't you help?" Another family was still waiting and wondering what happened to their daughter.

It was too early to check into my hotel when I arrived so I drove around Kirkland Lake for a bit, getting the sense that the town still had that "little rough around the edges" feel to it. Like many towns in Ontario it had the usual bingo hall, hockey rink and Royal Canadian Legion, bookended by two Tim Hortons donut shops. Chatting with a few locals over lunch at a pizzeria, I found out that in the early 1900s the town had literally been built on gold and the area had some of the richest gold mines in the world. They were equally proud of having produced a handful of hockey players who went on to play in the NHL. During the gold boom the town swelled to a population of twenty-five thousand from the more than thirty area mines, but now it was only about eight thousand.

After lunch I drove out to where Harvey Kirkland Road extended south from town and into the bush. Pavement turned into gravel and less than a kilometre into the pine bush was a clearing and small cluster of homes. The house that Kathy Wilson had lived in had long since burned down, but I found the address and retraced the route Kathy would have taken into town.

The next day Yvan Godin came with me to visit the only still-living members of the Wilson family, Kathy's seventy-six-year-old mother and her little sister, Pee Wee, fifty. (Karen Wilson had died of a heart attack only a few months earlier.) We met at Aline's apartment in town. There was more laughter than tears with stories of their early lives in Harvey Kirkland.

Pee Wee talked about what it was like to get the early-morning phone call from Yvan telling her that her cousin had finally been arrested. "It was better than winning a million," she said. "I phoned Karen and then we went to tell Mom. I was so excited when I got there that Mom actually thought that we had won the lottery because we had bought some tickets just a few days before."

Our conversation turned more serious when Aline recounted

the day that Kathy went missing and how the investigation had initially been bungled. Once filled with so much ill feeling toward the police, she now had nothing but praise for all that the OPP did for their family. She told me that although she would have done anything to get her daughter back alive, she would die in peace knowing what happened to Kathy. She confided then that she had terminal cancer, and she passed away a few months after we spoke.

When driving into Kirkland Lake to first meet the Wilsons, I had stopped to look at a beautiful memorial to the more than 1,700 miners who had died in area mining accidents since 1914. The memorial was located in the middle of a small park with picnic tables nearby to sit and reflect on what had occurred to so many miners in the past and to honour their legacy. The names of each of the mines and the year and number of deaths were recorded on three magnificent granite headstones. Next to them was a monument with five life-sized bronze miner figures. Local artists designed and built the forty-ton, thirty-three-foot-high structure made of black granite at an estimated cost of $365,000.

Before I left Kirkland Lake to return home, I drove northeast of town on a gravel road for about twelve kilometres through dense woods of pine and spruce. I stopped at a clearing in the trees about the size of a football field. On the north side, barely visible through tall grass, was another beautiful memorial. This one was only about six feet square and framed in white, foot-high, vinyl garden edging. Inside was a homemade wooden cross on a tilt, faded plastic and silk bouquets of flowers, weather-beaten teddy bears, tattered silk butterflies atop sticks of wood, along with washed-out black and white photographs and poems in dollar store–type frames. Just outside the edging was a small stone ground marker inscribed, "Kathy Wilson 1958–1970." Yvan Godin had bought the picnic table beside the memorial, a place where family and friends of Kathy had to come and sit and reflect on all that had happened at that location so many years ago.

NOT THE LAST CHAPTER

*"For retirement brings repose, and repose allows
a kindly judgment of all things."*
—John Sharp Williams

IN EARLY FEBRUARY 2010, I TRAVELLED to Belleville, Ontario, for what would be my last meeting with investigators who had at one time thought that all of their hard work and long hours would result in finding a missing young woman. I once again hoped my presence and words of support and encouragement would help them deal with their disappointment over the worst-possible outcome despite their efforts.

Marie-France Comeau, thirty-eight, a corporal at Canadian Forces Base Trenton, had been murdered in her home several months earlier. Another area resident, Jessica Lloyd, twenty-seven, had been missing from her home since January 28. Weeks earlier there had been two sexual assaults in the same area with similar modus operandi. On Thursday, February 4, the ViCLAS Unit was putting the final touches on linking all of the cases together back in Orillia, when at the same time a roadblock was set up near where Jessica lived, canvassing for information and possible witnesses. An SUV came through with tires that appeared to match tire prints taken near Jessica's home. The vehicle was driven by Russell Williams, a part-time resident of the nearby village of Tweed and base commander of CFB Trenton.

Over the next several days the investigative team scrambled to get search warrants prepared for Williams's Tweed home and the one he shared with his wife in Orleans, on the outskirts of Ottawa. All the while, he was under the twenty-four-hour watchful eye of mobile surveillance teams. Jim Smyth was summoned to Ottawa and when all the legal documents were signed and ready to go, he cold-called Williams at his Orleans home to request he come in for an interview. Williams didn't ask any questions and showed up about half an hour later. While Williams at first feigned innocence, about four and a half hours into the interview Jim finally persuaded the colonel that the evidence against him was irrefutable. Williams confessed to the unsolved sexual assaults and the murders of Marie Comeau and Jessica Lloyd. He also identified the location of Jessica's body and revealed where officers could find hidden evidence of these and other crimes.

Given William's profession, the investigative team was in the international media spotlight for weeks following his arrest. It occurred all over again when Williams pleaded guilty to all eighty-eight charges—two counts of murder, two counts of break and enter and sexual assault, two counts of forcible confinement; and eighty-two counts of break, enter and theft, most of which involved stealing women's and children's underwear. He was sentenced to life in prison.

My office in Orillia was now on the third floor of headquarters with one full wall of windows providing the best view in the building—overlooking Lake Simcoe. A "me" wall no longer took up any space on my walls. I was at that "I am what I am, take me or leave me" stage in my career and no longer felt the need to hang my training certificates or "attagirl" plaques to impress. Along with the now-faded photo of Mr. De Niro, they'd all long been packed away in boxes and replaced with artwork and photographs of my family, including my stepdaughter, Cheryl, her husband and my two stepgrandchildren, whom I had stayed close with over the years. Most of my time was now spent doing paperwork or attending meetings trying to keep all the balls in the air with over five hundred uniform and civilian full-time and contract employees working throughout Ontario. There were the usual operational and HR issues to deal with, but I found most of my time was taken up with challenges related to managing an annual budget of over $45 million. (It bears stressing that, given the rough time I had with numbers while working in Anti-Rackets Branch years earlier, having a crackerjack financial assistant was a key component to the job.)

With more than thirty years of police service and over the age of fifty, I'd been eligible for a comfortable retirement pension for the last three years. Although I'd spent more than half of my life as a cop, it had never felt like it was the right time for me to hang up my uniform. That changed when a twenty-three-year-old

OPP recruit walked into my office at the end of April. He'd dropped by to personally thank me for mentoring him through phone calls and emails over the last five or so years as he prepared himself for a career in policing. Luke Robillard was actually my cousin but we had never met before as he lived hundreds of miles away in Dryden, Ontario. We only talked for about a half hour but I knew he would make a great cop. He was mature for his years, well educated with the bonus of street smarts and, without a doubt, was motivated to succeed.

Before Luke left that day he asked me if I would present him with his badge at his graduation ceremony a few months later. At that moment I knew I'd found my right time to make my exit gracefully. If I was going to pass a torch to the next generation of officers, this was the guy I wanted to give it to. On September 10, 2010, I attended Luke's graduation and presented him with his badge—it was my last assignment on my last day as a police officer.

Each of my career postings had their own unique challenges and those that I initially struggled with provided me with some of my greatest satisfaction. I was most proud of achieving the number of Canadian firsts in the multidisciplinary Behavioural Sciences Section and all its various units. I am particularly honoured and touched that each year since I'd left BSS they've given out an annual award for leadership in my name.

I'd left BSS in good hands. With the establishment of the Ontario ViCLAS Centre in 1996, all cases meeting ViCLAS criteria were analyzed daily and compared to other similar crimes across Canada in an effort to identify suspects and serial offenders, such as David Snow, Paul Bernardo and Russell Williams, at the earliest opportunity. There were over 185,000 cases on the Ontario database and 479,000 on the national database. ViCLAS was now used for crime linkage analysis by police in Belgium, Czech Republic, France, Germany, Ireland, Netherlands, New Zealand, Switzerland and the United Kingdom, resulting in success stories around the world.

Since the 2006 launch of the Missing Persons and Unidentified Bodies website, fifty-six missing persons and nineteen unidentified remains cases were solved either directly by the MPUB Unit, or by way of them passing on tips and information to investigating police agencies. One of the solved unidentified human remains cases dated back to 1968. The faces of missing children, like Michael Dunahee, Kristen French, Leslie Mahaffy, Christopher Stephenson, Tori Stafford and Kathy Wilson were no longer plastered on milk cartons, the back of commercial trucks, or mailed out to neighbouring communities on posters. Many cases were cracked with the assistance of members of the public accessing our Internet site and providing tips that led to locating a missing person or identifying a deceased person. Some cases had the best possible outcome and reconnections with family members and friends were facilitated by police. In other cases, searchers were advised that the person they were looking for had been located but didn't want their contact information or whereabouts given to the searcher. Their right to privacy always prevailed. And for those deceased persons who were subsequently identified, like Russell Pensyl, there were no happy endings, but at least some level of closure for family and friends. (Following Ontario's lead, in 2013 the federal government opened a National Centre for Missing Persons and Unidentified Remains, operated by the RCMP.)

The Ontario Sex Offender Registry today holds over 17,000 files for 158 Ontario police agencies to directly access. Offender-residence information is not released to the public as do some registries in the United States and elsewhere and I am confident this is one of the reasons why our offender registration compliance averages 98 percent. (It's important to note that Ontario police chiefs have authority under other provincial legislation to notify the public of persons who pose a risk to public safety. Police are unobtrusively keeping track of them above ground, and if any do go underground, they use whatever means possible to find them.) Although Canada's national registry was established in 2004, Ontario continues to operate its own due to its additional features not available with the national registry, such as direct database access by police agencies.

The Threat Assessment Unit was receiving over three hundred cases annually, involving such crimes as domestic, school and workplace violence, as well as all types of harassment. More and more cases demonstrated the dangerousness of social networking websites and oversharing personal information. The officers assigned to the unit were recognized for their expertise in victim safety planning and also for providing threat/risk assessment at all levels of court in Ontario, testifying at bail, sentencing and dangerous offender hearings. Working with the Research Unit and mental health professionals, they developed the Ontario Domestic Assault Risk Assessment (ODARA) tool, an empirically validated risk assessment tool that provided a risk level for recidivism in partner assaults. The ODARA was now used across Canada, as well as the US, New Zealand, Switzerland and Austria.

The Research Unit was a sought-after collaborator by some of the most prestigious research institutions in North America. Partners included the University of California (threats against justice officials), Waypoint Centre for Mental Health Care (domestic violence), Royal Ottawa Health Care Centre (child pornography and child sexual exploitation) and Centre for Addiction and Mental Health (offender recidivism). Their findings were published in high-impact journals, and cited in court cases, policy statements, etc., all over the world. It naturally followed that their research was relevant to the criminal justice community as a whole, including mental health practitioners for assessment and treatment, as well as probation and parole officers when supervising offenders after their release. All were benefiting from a better understanding of criminal motivation and violent, or potentially violent, criminal behaviour.

The expertise of the Criminal Profiling Unit had expanded to respond to emerging crime trends such as terrorism, gang violence and cybercrimes. They regularly hosted profiling understudies from police agencies around the world who not only came to the OPP for practical experience working cases with profilers, but also to gain insight into the other behavioural science support services offered.

The OPP had 6100 uniform police officers and 1200 of them were women. Alongside their brother officers they worked in highly specialized areas such as criminal profiling, polygraph, forensic identification, underwater search and rescue, electronic crime, child pornography, wiretaps, and were in charge of uniform officers and civilians in detachments and regional command centres across the province. They had volunteered for United Nations assignments in places like Haiti, Sudan/South Sudan, Kosovo, East Timor, Jordan and Lebanon. A policewoman was the ride master of the OPP's Golden Helmets Motorcycle Precision Team. Women in the OPP knew there were limitless opportunities for them to pursue their dream jobs and promotions to the highest rank, including commissioner. When the next woman fills that position, she will follow in the footsteps of Gwen Boniface who in 1998 became the OPP's twelfth commissioner, and first woman to achieve the rank.

My retirement didn't last long. Although it was nice to be away from the winter cold, six months living in a retirement community in Florida was enough rumination time for me. Plus I'd had my fill of pool exercise classes to the tunes of Barbra Streisand, early-bird dinner specials and bingo as my evening's entertainment.

When I got back home in the spring I decided to reboot and start up my own consulting business, as well as get my private investigator's licence. (In Ontario if you want to be an investigator for hire you have to pass a fifty-hour course to get your licence—pretty easy for us ex-cops, as long as you don't forget you're not carrying a badge anymore.) I knew my behavioural sciences and profiling background would be useful to more than just those in the policing business.

My second career involves a variety of investigation and interviewing assignments for private, corporate and government clients. My assignments involve allegations of everything from child abduction and abuse to harassment, human rights violations, threatening, and violence in the workplace. I balance those with speaking engagements and teaching in-class and online courses in criminal investigative analysis and investigative interviewing. I've also remained active in volunteering for victim justice initiatives, not-for-profit fundraisers and talking at recruitment initiatives that encourage women and men to consider careers in policing.

Given the popularity of criminal profiling, over the years I've appeared in documentaries and fact-based TV shows like *Exhibit A* and *Murder She Solved*, as well as consulted with authors on their books and scriptwriters for TV shows such as *Flashpoint* and *Rookie Blue*. While I often get asked to be a media commentator for various real-time network news programs, these are the types of requests I always decline. Being a boutique profiler speculating on someone else's unfolding criminal investigation, without having all the facts at my disposal, is not something I am interested in doing.

I consider it an obligation and necessity to keep my skills up to date in my new, self-managed career. I hadn't attended a Quantico in-service in more than a decade and in 2014 the perfect opportunity presented itself: a professional week-long program that not only hosted profilers, but also researchers, investigative and forensic psychiatrists and psychologists from Canada, the US, Australia and Netherlands. Just like the old days, our agenda included updates on the latest behavioural analysis techniques, research and solved case reviews, as well as the opportunity for visiting police to present violent-crime cases for profiling assistance.

Three of my 1990–91 fellowship classmates made up the more than fifty of us in attendance. The BSU had long since moved out of the basement of the Academy to an off-site office location south of Quantico, but a number of their members returned and sat in with us each day. Later in the week we were joined for dinner by some of our original instructors to celebrate the thirtieth anniversary of the ICIAF—Judson Ray, Gregg McCrary, Ken Lanning and Roy Hazelwood among them. I was also thrilled to make the acquaintance of seventy-six-year-old Roger Depue, the first BSU chief and the one responsible for establishing the FBI's police fellowship training. I was grateful to be able to shake his hand and personally thank him for setting the stage for not only one, but two, of the best careers a girl could have.

ACKNOWLEDGEMENTS

To now-retired OPP commissioner Chris Lewis, my heartfelt gratitude for his early and lasting support of this book. I am indebted to the many men and women of the OPP, FBI, other law enforcement agencies and all those who helped me to stay on track with my story facts and keep my memories upright.

I want to express my deepest appreciation to the victims and/or their families for giving me permission to share their tragedies and how I came to be involved in them. Thank you to Bruce and Crystal Dunahee, Doug and Donna French, Sheldon Kennedy, Jim and Anna Stephenson, Tara McDonald, Rodney Stafford, Aline and Pee Wee Wilson, and Jen. In particular, thank you to Orville and Susan Osbourne for allowing me to also share the graphic details of the murders of Ian and Nancy Blackburn in order to help explain how my work on their case was done. All of you are wonderful examples of courage and strength.

I never could have imagined the cathartic experience writing this book would be for me. Award-winning writer and friend Stevie Cameron persuaded me to tell my story the way I wanted to tell it—with the sensationalism battened down. I loved my job as much the day I retired as the day I was hired and I am so glad that Stevie convinced me that people would be interested to know why. Thank you to Louise Dennys and Marion Garner of Penguin Random House for taking a chance on me and particularly to my editor, Pamela Murray, for her patience, encouragement and guidance. I know it was not an easy job trying to turn this "just the facts" cop into a writer.

Whatever I have achieved personally or professionally in my life, I would not have without the love and support of family and friends. Mom, Gerry, Barb, Bo, J.D., Cheryl, Wayne and the rest of our clan—thank you for always being there. Police padre, Father Bob Hale—what a joy to have had you and your Rochester crew in my life. And to my "Ya Yas" and "Titunas"— you are simply the best.

NOTES

1. http://www.heritagemississauga.com/page/Mississauga-Train-Derailment

2. http://www.missingkids.com/en_US/publications/NC70.pdf

3. http://www.atg.wa.gov/uploadedFiles/Another/Supporting_Law_ Enforcement/Homicide_Investigation_Tracking_System_%28HITS%29/ Child_Abduction_Murder_Research/CMIIPDF.pdf, page 13.

4. http://archive.constantcontact.com/fs037/1102448202986/archive/ 1103344752665.html

5. Utility of unknown offender profile in serial predator investigations investigation can be found at http://www.opconline.ca/depts/omcm/ Campbell/Bernardo_Investigation_Review%20PDF.pdf, page 156.

6. August 24, 2012 interview and other communications with RCMP officer Larry Wilson.

7. FBI profile of Scarborough rapist found at: www.opconline.ca/depts/ omcm/Campbell/Bernardo_Investigation_Review%20PDF.pdf, Appendix 3, page 365.

8. Personal correspondence

9. Personal correspondence

10. "Microsoft Collaborates With Global Police to Develop Child Exploitation Tracking System for Law Enforcement Agencies," Microsoft News Center, April 07, 2005. www.microsoft.com/en-us/news/press/ 2005/apr05/04-07cetspr.aspx

11. icaremissingpersonscoldcases.yuku.com/

12. www.missing-u.ca/ British Columbia joined the initiative in 2008. (At press the OPP was transitioning all of its cases to the new National Centre for Missing Persons and Unidentified Remains website at www.canadasmissing.ca)

SOURCES

Barnes, Michael. *Policing Ontario: The OPP Today*. Erin, Ontario: Boston Mills Press, 1991.

Brussel, James A., *Casebook of a Crime Psychiatrist*. New York: Bernard Geis Associates, 1968.

Campbell, Justice Archie. "Bernardo Investigation Review." Ontario Ministry of the Solicitor General and Correctional Services,1996.

Campbell, John H. and Don DeNevi, editors. *Profilers:Leading Investigators Take You Inside the Criminal Mind*. New York: Prometheus Books, 2004.

Clark, Doug. *Dark Paths, Cold Trails*. Toronto: HarperCollins Publishers Ltd., 2002.

DeNevi, Don and John H. Campbell, *Into the Minds of Madmen*. Amherst: Prometheus Books, 2004.

Depue, Roger L. with Susan Schindehette. *Between Good and Evil*. New York: Warner Books, 2005.

Douglas, John and Mark Olshaker. *Mind Hunter*. New York: Scribner, 1995.

Douglas, John and Mark Olshaker. *Journey Into Darkness*. New York: Scribner, 1997.

Douglas, John and Mark Olshaker. *Obsession*. New York: Scribner, 1998.

Douglas, John and Mark Olshaker. *The Anatomy of Motive*. New York: Scribner, 1999.

Green, Valerie. *Vanished: The Michael Dunahee Story*. Surrey, BC: Hancock House Publishers, 2012.

Groth, A. Nicholas. *Men Who Rape: The Psychology of the Offender*. New York: Plenum Press, 1979.

Hazelwood, Roy and Ann Wolf Burgess. *Practical Aspects of Rape Investigation: A Multidisciplinary Approach*, 4th Edition. Boca Raton: CRC Press, 2009.

Hazelwood, Roy with Stephen G. Michaud. *Dark Dreams: Sexual Violence, Homicide and The Criminal Mind*. New York: St. Martin's Press, 2001.

icaremissingpersonscoldcases.yuku.com

Kaufman, Fred, C.M, Q.C. "Report of the Kaufman Commission on Proceedings Involving Guy Paul Morin." Ontario Ministry of the Attorney General, 1997.

Kennedy, Sheldon and James Grainger. *Why I Didn't Say Anything: The Sheldon Kennedy Story.* Toronto: Insomniac Press, 2006.

Matthews, Jennifer. *A Century of Policing: The Ontario Provincial Police, 1909–2009.* Toronto: Ontario Provincial Police, 2009.

McCrary, Gregg O. with Katherine Ramsland. *The Unknown Darkness.* New York: HarperCollins, 2003.

Michaud, Stephen G. with Roy Hazelwood. *The Evil That Men Do.* New York: St. Martin's Press, 1999.

National Center for the Analysis of Violent Crime. *Criminal Investigative Analysis: Sexual Homicide.* Quantico: FBI Academy, 1990.

National Center for the Analysis of Violent Crime. *Deviant and Criminal Sexuality*, 2nd Edition. Quantico: FBI Academy, 1993.

Ressler, Robert K., Ann W. Burgess and John E. Douglas. *Sexual Homicide: Patterns and Motives.* New York: The Free Press, 1992.

Shaw, Alison. *A Friend of the Family: The True Story of David Snow.* Toronto: Macfarlane Walter & Ross, 1998.

The Abduction of Kristen French," CHCH-TV. Niagara Television Limited, Hamilton, Ontario. July 21, 1992.

www.canadasmissing.ca

www.cbc.ca/archives/categories/society/crime-justice/cold-cases-unsolved -crimes-in-canada/michael-dunahee-victoria-1991.html

www.fbi.gov/about-us/cirg/investigations-and-operations-support/briu

www.heritagemississauga.com/page/Mississauga-Train-Derailment

www.missingkids.com

www.missing-u.ca

www.opp.ca

INDEX

KATE LINES joined the Ontario Provincial Police in 1977. Her early days at work comprised uniform patrol, undercover drugs, fraud and major crimes. In 1991, she completed the FBI's Criminal Profiling Fellowship Program in Quantico, Virginia, the second Canadian to graduate from the program. Lines later became the first female Director of Intelligence Bureau. Much honoured during her thirty-three-year policing career, Lines received the Officer of the Order of Merit Medal, Queen's Commission, International Association of Women Police Excellence in Performance Award, Ontario Women in Law Enforcement Excellence in Performance and Team Endeavours Award and Canadian Police Leadership Forum's Police Leader of the Year Award. She currently acts as a consultant to businesses and police forces and on TV shows such as *Rookie Blue* and *Flashpoint*.